THE LAW (

Please return/renew this item by the date it is due back. Charges will be made for items returned late. Items can be renewed by telephone or via "e-library." Just go to www.bexley.gov.uk/library. You will need your library card number and PIN. You can also use "e-library" to search the library catalogue and reserve items.

Central Library
02083037777

LONDON BOROUGH OF
BEXLEY

553009/1.08

The Law of
Mobile Homes and
Caravans

SECOND EDITION

by
Paul Clayden
M.A. (Oxon.), Solicitor

Shaw & Sons

Published by
Shaw & Sons Limited
Shaway House
21 Bourne Park
Bourne Road
Crayford
Kent DA1 4BZ

www.shaws.co.uk

© Shaw & Sons Limited 2003

First Edition......................January 1985
Second Edition..................... May 2003

ISBN 0 7219 0812 8

Printed in Great Britain by
Bell & Bain Limited, Glasgow

CONTENTS

PREFACE

This is a new edition of a book originally written by Richard Gordon and first published in 1978 under the title *Caravans and the Law* and revised in 1985 as *The Law Relating to Mobile Homes and Caravans*, in order to highlight the fact that, in law, there is no differentiation between a mobile home and a caravan.

Whilst the main statutory provisions relating directly to mobile homes and caravans have not altered a great deal in the intervening years, there have been many changes in law, practice and policy in related areas. The main changes which have taken place are: (1) the abolition of the duty on local authorities to provide sites for travellers (abolished by section 60 of the Criminal Justice and Public Order Act 1994); (2) new laws relating to the removal of unauthorised campers (sections 77-79 of the 1994 Act); (3) new security of tenure provisions for residential tenants in the Housing Acts 1988 and 1996.

The Government of Wales Act 1998 established the National Assembly for Wales, to which most of the functions of the Secretary of State for Wales were transferred by the National Assembly for Wales (Transfer of Functions) Order 1999 (S.I. 1999 No. 672). The Order transferred the powers of the Secretary of State in relation to caravans and mobile homes with effect from 1st July 1999.

Crown Copyright material is reproduced under the terms of Crown Copyright Policy Guidance issued by Her Majesty's Stationery Office.

Paul Clayden
Henley-on-Thames

TABLE OF STATUTES

TABLE OF STATUTORY INSTRUMENTS

TABLE OF CASES

ABBREVIATIONS

Acts of Parliament and other abbreviations referred to in this book are as follows:

"the 1960 Act"	the Caravan Sites and Control of Development Act 1968
"the 1968 Act"	the Caravan Sites Act 1968
"the 1983 Act"	the Mobile Homes Act 1983
"the 1990 Act"	the Town and Country Planning Act 1990
"the EPA 1990"	the Environmental Protection Act 1990
"the 1994 Act"	the Criminal Justice and Public Order Act 1994.
"the CPR"	the Civil Procedure Rules 1998 (S.I. 1998 No. 3132, as amended)
"DOE"	the former Department of the Environment
"PPG"	Planning Policy Guidance Notes issued by the Office of the Deputy Prime Minister (the government department primarily responsible for town and country planning matters)
"TCP"	Town and Country Planning
"WO"	the Welsh Office

INTRODUCTION

Chapter 1

A BRIEF HISTORY OF CARAVAN CONTROL PRIOR TO 1960

The legislative provisions relating to caravans and mobile homes are considered in detail in Parts I to IV of this book. At this stage, however, it is important to know something of the background to that legislation in order to understand how and why certain measures become necessary.

The Early Caravan Dwellers

The earliest inhabitants of caravans[1] came, in general, from the poorest sections of society. They comprised, for the most part, poor wayfarers, nomads and similar members of the community.

In some respects the problems faced by such persons were similar to those facing gypsies today.[2] The conditions under which they lived were (even by contemporary standards) far lower than those of the majority of the population. The public health hazards that these conditions created were largely ignored until the late nineteenth century. Instead, the so-called "vagabonds" were subjected to harsh restrictions under the vagrancy laws in an effort to prevent the squalor in which they lived from spreading to the rest of the country.

After the passing of the Reform Act in 1832 much more attention was devoted to matters relating to public health and social improvement. Apart from a thorough overhaul of the Poor Law system (which had prevailed since Elizabethan times), there was in the 1840s increased public concern over the question of health.

---

[1]   There are recorded instances of caravans in England during the Stuart period.
[2]   See ch. 13.

Two major reports on the Sanitary Condition of the Labouring Population (1842) and the State of Large Towns (1845) revealed the appalling squalor and filth in which most of the working and urban population lived. There followed a spate of public health legislation, culminating in the Public Health Act of 1875. Praiseworthy as it was, however, none of the legislation enacted during this period affected caravan dwellers at all. In particular, efforts to deal with the living conditions of the labouring populace concentrated on those workers who had dwelling houses rather than those who led a nomadic existence.[3]

It was not until the Housing of the Working Classes Act was passed in 1885 that the law concerned itself with the problems of caravan accommodation. Section 9 of that Act applied to "tents, vans, sheds and similar structures used for human habitation".[4] It contained provisions for preventing and dealing with nuisances arising from such structures by reason of overcrowding, lack of adequate sanitary accommodation, etc.

Although the 1885 Act was essentially prohibitory in character, it represented a genuine attempt to remedy health hazards in caravans. Some of its provisions remain effectively in force today.[5] Unfortunately, however, the Act was based on a premise which was soon to be eroded, namely that all persons who lived in caravans were vagrants and, therefore, liable to cause public health risks. That assumption may have been valid when the Act was passed but, by the early twentieth century, it was apparent that this was no longer so.

Public Health Licences
In the 1920s and 1930s a new type of caravan dweller began to emerge. The increasing popularity of caravanning

---

[3]   *Cf.* the Labouring Classes Dwelling Houses Acts 1866 and 1867, and the Artizans and Labourers Dwellings Act 1868.
[4]   *Cf.* the more modern definition of "caravan"; see ch. 3.
[5]   Substantially repeated in s. 268 of the Public Health Act 1936.

as a leisure pastime broadened the class of persons who regularly used caravans. It meant that, in a growing number of cases, residents of caravans were respectable people who could be trusted not to cause health risks. These were often the very people to be convicted in magistrates' courts of offences under out of date vagrancy laws because of the difficulty of pitching their caravans on properly authorised sites.

The Public Health Act of 1936 was, in part, an attempt to distinguish between the new type of caravan dweller and the vagrant. Section 269 thereof created a system of licensing which required the occupier of land who wished to permit it to be used for camping purposes for more than sixty days a year (or forty-two consecutive days) to obtain a licence from the local authority. In certain cases it was also necessary for the caravan occupant himself to obtain a licence.[6] The effect of the section was to place strict public health controls over vagrants who used their caravans on a permanent basis, but to encourage casual holiday caravanning.

In addition, section 268 of the 1936 Act, apart from re-enacting substantially section 9 of the Housing of the Working Classes Act 1885, applied other parts of the Act to caravans so as to give local authorities increased powers and duties in matters relating to public health.[7] The provisions of section 268 (and other parts of that Act applied by it) still have effect, but section 269, insofar as it related to caravans, was repealed by section 30 of the Caravan Sites and Control of Development Act 1960.

Amenity Legislation
It was not until after the Second World War (and the housing shortage that it created) that caravans were viewed as a possible source of permanent accommodation by persons other than the traditional nomad.

---

[6] Public Health Act 1936, s. 269(3).
[7] See ch. 7.

In the immediate post-war years, sites were rapidly developed on a widespread basis to cater for the increasing number of families who, either by choice or necessity, wished to make their caravan into a permanent home.

The problems that this development created were considerable. Site owners were anxious to fill their land – often without regard to considerations of amenity or public health. As caravans became more numerous and larger (through adaptation for permanent accommodation) these problems intensified.

There were, as we have seen, effective public health safeguards at this time. It was, however, not possible for local authorities, under the existing scheme of control, to take steps to prevent residential sites from causing detriment to the amenities of a neighbourhood. In *Pilling v. Abergele U.D.C.*[8] it was expressly held that a local authority were not entitled to refuse a site licence under the Public Health Act 1936 because amenities might be impaired.

The Town and Country Planning Act 1947, which came into effect on 18th July 1948, introduced a system of planning control whereby the consent of the local planning authority had to be obtained in respect of most kinds of "development" of land (as defined by the Act).

So far as caravans were concerned, the usual type of development requiring planning permission was that involving what was termed "a material change" in the use of any land. In general, establishing a caravan site did constitute a material change of use and planning consent was therefore required. There were certain exceptions to this,[9] particularly where use could be established prior to the passing of the Act.

The basic ideas of the 1947 Act have been repeated in

---

[8]   [1950] 1 All E.R. 76.
[9]   Planning permission is now a prerequisite to the granting of a site licence; see ch. 3.

subsequent legislation.[10] The present Town and Country Planning Act of 1990 contains a slightly different procedure and gives increased powers to the authority responsible for planning control.[11] It enacts, however, substantially the same law and the criteria for the granting or withholding of planning permission are the same now as they were under the original Act of 1947.

---

[10] i.e. the T. & C.P. Acts of 1962, 1968, 1971 and 1990.
[11] See ch. 4.

Chapter 2

THE SCOPE OF THE CURRENT LAW

After the passing of The Town and Country Planning Act of 1947 there were two distinct systems of control over public health and amenity hazards presented by caravan accommodation. Unfortunately, however, these controls operated independently of each other. Planning permission might well be granted for development only to be rendered ineffective by the refusal of a site licence on public health grounds. Alternatively, a site licence might be granted but planning permission withheld. An unnecessary wasting of time was involved on the part of the site owner and local authority alike.

By 1960, it was apparent that further legislation would be required to improve the two forms of control. It was not fully appreciated then that, with the growing popularity of caravans as residences, it would also be necessary to give a measure of protection to caravan dwellers in terms of security of tenure and terms of occupancy similar to that provided under the newly emerging Rent Act legislation (consolidated into the Rent Act 1977 and now largely replaced by the Housing Acts 1988 and 1996 – see Chapter 12).

As a result, the current law relating to caravans and mobile homes has tended to develop on a piecemeal basis with different Acts being passed to cover different aspects of the same problem.

The Principal Statutes
There are now three principal statutes regulating the use of land for caravans and the terms of occupancy thereof. They are:

(1) The Caravan Sites and Control of Development Act 1960.

(2) The Caravan Sites Act 1968.

(3) The Mobile Homes Act 1983.

(1) The Caravan Sites and Control of Development Act 1960
Part I of this Act provides for a system of licensing of
caravan sites. It is much more closely linked with the
planning control system and, in effect, makes the two
forms of control interdependent.

The Act establishes a scheme involving the granting of
"site licences" which may only be issued after planning
permission has been obtained in respect of the relevant
land. There is provision for prior consultation between
the planning authority and the authority responsible for
issuing the site licence.[1]

In addition, the 1960 Act gives to local authorities certain
powers in relation to sites enabling them to provide
caravan sites and to manage those sites or lease them to
others. There is also power to prohibit caravanning on
commons in certain circumstances.[2]

(2) The Caravan Sites Act 1968
Part I of the Act contains provisions designed to give the
permanent caravan dweller protection against eviction
and harassment.[3] The provisions do little more than
require a site owner to give four weeks' notice to quit and,
thereafter, to obtain a court order for possession. The Act,
however, gives a basic measure of protection against
summary eviction and harassment on the part of the site
owner. The court has power to suspend a possession order
for a limited period.

Part II, which placed a duty on local authorities to provide

---

[1]   See chs. 3 and 5. Part II of the 1960 Act has been repealed by
       subsequent Town and Country Planning legislation.
[2]   See ch. 7.
[3]   See chs. 8 and 9.

caravan sites for gypsies, was repealed by the Criminal Justice and Public Order Act 1994.[4]

(3) The Mobile Homes Act 1983
The purpose of the Act is to supplement Part I of the 1968 Act by providing increased security of tenure. The Act also provides for site owners to give written details of agreements to mobile home owners and implies certain terms in such agreements.

The 1983 Act does not apply to mobile homes that are rented, rather than owned, nor does it apply to holiday caravans or to floating houseboats.[5] It does, however, apply to sites owned by local authorities.

Other Legislation Affecting Caravans

The three statutes referred to constitute, together, a unified body of law solely concerned with caravan control and occupancy.

There are, however, certain other Acts that relate to caravans and which will be considered in this book insofar as they have a bearing on the subject.

(1) Planning
As has been stated, site licence control is now closely linked with planning control.

The Town and Country Planning Act 1990 contains provisions dealing with the grant and enforcement of planning permission. As such they are of importance in the context of caravan law. Also important is the Town and Country Planning (General Permitted Development) Order 1995, as amended, which gives detailed guidance on aspects of planning procedure, such as forms of application, publicity for applications, etc.[6]

---

4   See ch. 14.
5   *Chelsea Yacht & Boat Co. Ltd. v. Pope* [2000] 1 W.L.R. 1941.
6   See chs. 4 and 6.

(2) Building Regulations

In some instances, a mobile home may constitute a "building" for the purpose of certain building regulations.[7]

(3) Public Health

Although most aspects of public health will now be covered by conditions imposed under a caravan site licence, local authorities have residual powers under section 268 of the Public Health Act 1936, and under both Part III of the Environmental Protection Act 1990 and the various parts of the 1936 Act expressly incorporated by the section.[8]

(4) Council Tax and Non-Domestic Rating

The occupiers of residential caravans and mobile homes are generally liable to pay council tax, as provided for in the Local Government Finance Act 1992 and its subordinate legislation. There are special rules relating to "leisure caravans" as defined in the Rating (Caravan Sites) Act 1976 and the Non-domestic Rating (Caravan Sites) Regulations 1990 (S.I. 1990 No. 673). In general, leisure caravan sites are liable to non-domestic rates rather than council tax.[9]

(5) Road Traffic

All caravans liable to be conveyed on public roads are subject to control under the Road Traffic Act 1988 and regulations made pursuant to the Act. In practice, it is in the Motor Vehicles (Construction and Use) Regulations 1986 (as amended) that most of the detailed requirements relating to caravans are to be found.[10]

(6) Taxation

As a general rule, no tax relief is available for the interest on a loan taken out to buy a caravan or a mobile home (section 38 of the Finance Act 1999). The Value Added

---

[7]   See ch. 7, pp. 72-81.
[8]   See ch. 7.
[9]   See ch. 15.
[10]   See ch. 16.

Tax Act 1994 specifies the rate of value added tax on different types of caravan.[11]

(7) Capital Gains

Certain types of modern caravan amount, in law, to "dwelling houses". They may, in certain circumstances, be exempt from capital gains tax on resale.

---

[11] See ch. 17.

Part I

CARAVAN SITE CONTROL

Chapter 3

REQUIREMENTS AND DEFINITIONS

The Scheme of Control

The Caravan Sites and Control of Development Act 1960, which came into effect on 29th August 1960, introduced the present system of control of caravan sites.

By virtue of Part I of the Act, caravan sites are controlled, subject to important exceptions,[1] by a scheme of licensing. Site licences are issued by the local authority in whose area the particular site is situated.[2] In most cases licences are not difficult to obtain. The real measure of control, however, lies in the conditions that may be attached to the licence,[3] and in the powers available to the local authority for the enforcement of any conditions imposed.[4]

The licensing form of control operates in addition to the older, and more general, control of development through the requirement of planning permission that has already been referred to. The two forms of control, although distinct, are not exclusive. The criteria affecting the grant of planning permission are, in general, different from those that determine the nature of the conditions to be imposed under a particular site licence.[5] Nonetheless, the two systems, taken together, constitute a unified and interdependent method of control. This reciprocal

---

[1] See ch. 5.
[2] 1960 Act, s. 3. The definition of "local authority" in the 1960 Act is "a council of a London Borough or a district, the Common Council of the City of London and the Council of the Isles of Scilly but, in relation to Wales, means the council of a Welsh county or county borough".
[3] See ch. 5.
[4] See ch. 6.
[5] The licensing system is concerned with the internal arrangements of the site and deals with matters such as the numbers and types of caravans on the site. Planning considerations are different and are examined in ch. 4.

dependence is illustrated by the requirement that, before a site licence can be issued, planning permission must have already been granted for the site in question.

The Requirement for Planning Permission

Section 3(3) of the Act[6] provides that a local authority may, on an application for a site licence, issue such licence "if and only if" the applicant is, at the time when the site licence is issued, entitled to the benefit of a permission for the use of the land as a caravan site otherwise than by a development order.

Therefore, a formal grant of planning permission is a prerequisite for the issue of a site licence. If such permission is not granted, then the application for a site licence will be rejected. This will be the case whatever the reason for the failure to obtain planning permission. Where, for example, the use of the land as a caravan site does not involve development, it will still be necessary to apply for, and obtain, formal planning consent.

In this context it should be observed that it is not only the planning authority that may grant a permission so as to enable a site licence to be obtained: it is solely permission granted under a development order that is excluded from the terms of the section. It is possible, therefore, for the Secretary of State or an Inspector appointed by the Secretary of State to grant a valid planning permission[7] and, if he does so, a further application to the planning authority will not be required.

By way of contrast, once planning permission has been granted in the manner prescribed in section 3(3) of the Act, it usually follows that a site licence will be granted as a matter of course.

---

6   "The Act" in this chapter means the 1960 Act unless otherwise stated.
7   As where he upholds an appeal against the refusal of planning permission; see ch. 4.

The Requirement for a Site Licence

The obligation to obtain a licence, before land is used as a caravan site, is strict. Subject to certain exceptions, section 1(1) of the Act states that no occupier of land[8] should "cause or permit" any part of his land to be used as a caravan site unless he holds a current site licence in respect of the land.

An occupier who contravenes the section commits an offence and is liable, on conviction in the magistrates' court, to a maximum fine of Level 4 on the standard scale (currently £2,500).[9]

It is not always that an offence arises. For example, if a site licence should have been granted by the local authority there is no offence committed under section 1(1).[10] Moreover, an occupier is not bound to take steps which are manifestly unreasonable to prevent his land from being used as a caravan site without a licence. What amounts to unreasonableness is very much a question of fact, however, and no definite standards can be laid down.

The circumstances that arose in *Test Valley Investments Ltd. v. Tanner*[11] are instructive. In that case gypsies set up a caravan site which was occupied by a floating population of squatters. The defendant landowners did not consent to this use of their land and they eventually obtained an injunction against the gypsies. The injunction proved impossible to enforce and the local authority suggested that the defendants should personally evict the gypsies. When they failed to do so they were prosecuted for, and convicted of, an offence under the Public Health Act 1936. On appeal, the Divisional Court held that, in the circumstances, it was unreasonable to expect the

---

[8]   See p. 23.
[9]   1960 Act, s. 1(2).
[10] See p. 39 and 1960 Act, s. 6.
[11] (1964) 15 P. & C.R. 279. See also *Bromsgrove District Council v. Carthy* (1975) 30 P. & C.R. 34 (a case also involving gypsies).

defendants to use self help, which necessarily involved a certain amount of risk. They were not guilty of an offence after beginning proceedings for an injunction.

(The provisions relating to the eviction of unauthorised campers from land in Part V of the Criminal Justice and Public Order Act 1994 would probably now be operated in similar circumstances today.)

On similar principles, it is submitted that a site owner ought not to be expected to take steps to prevent his land from being used as a caravan site, contrary to section 1(1), that would amount to harassment under the Caravan Sites Act 1968 (for which see later). In *Dean Lane Park (Merstham) Ltd. v. Hedge*,[12] a County Court Judge granted an injunction preventing a site owner who had instituted proceedings for possession from cutting off water and other services pending trial of the action. It cannot be the law that a site owner is, by submitting to the terms of such injunction, committing an offence under section 1(1).

Where a site licence is required, the site is a "protected site" and the owner must provide the occupier of a mobile home on it with a written statement in accordance with section 1 of the 1983 Act (see below, page 113), even if no site licence has been obtained.[13]

Definition of "Caravan"

"Caravan" is defined in section 29(1) of the Act to mean "any structure designed or adapted for human habitation which is capable of being moved from one place to another (whether by being towed, or by being transported on a motor vehicle or trailer), and any motor vehicle so designed or adapted".

In *Carter v. Secretary of State for the Environment* [1994] 1 W.L.R. 1212, a "park home" consisting of prefabricated

---

[12]   (1968) 208 *Estates Gazette* 149.
[13]   *Brice v. National By-Products; National By-Products v. Brice* (1983) 81 L.G.R. 652; *The Times*, 19 February 1983.

sections was delivered to site by a lorry. The sections were then dragged on to a concrete base. The structure had no wheels. C. claimed entitlement to an established use certificate on the basis that the previous structure on the site had been a caravan. The Court of Appeal held that the structure did not fall within the definition of a caravan in section 29 of the 1960 Act and C. could not therefore rely on the presence of the previously sited caravan to justify his claim for an established use certificate.

In *Howard v. Charlton* [2002] *The Times*, 19 August, the Court of Appeal held that the addition of a bolt-on porch extension 3.1 metres by 1.9 metres to one side of a mobile home did not result in the mobile home ceasing to be mobile and thus falling outside the ambit of the 1983 Act.

Specifically excluded from the definition of "caravan", however, are:

(i) railway rolling stock which is, for the time being, on rails, forming part of a railway system;

(ii) tents.

It will be seen that the definition incorporates certain structures not ordinarily identified as caravans in the popular imagination. Thus, for example, a camper van or autohome would come within the ambit of the section. On the other hand, a motor vehicle (a Commer van) which, although capable of being lived in, was not designed or had not been physically altered for that purpose has been held not to be a caravan.[14]

Not all caravans fall within the statutory scheme of control. A houseboat which is moored to the verge of a protected site is not a caravan stationed on it for the purpose of section 1 of the Act (see page 22), although it is in most cases a caravan within the meaning of section 29.[15]

---

[14] *Backer v. Secretary of State for the Environment* [1983] 2 All E.R. 1021.
[15] *Roy Crimble Ltd. v. Edgecombe* (1981) 131 N.L.J. 928, C.A.

The modern mobile home is virtually immobile[16] and there was initial uncertainty as to whether the above definition included such larger units which are often manufactured and transported in two parts although they can, if necessary, be transported as a whole.

Section 29 has been extended by the Caravan Sites Act 1968[17] so as to include twin unit caravans provided that such structures, when assembled, are:

(a) composed of not more than two separately constructed sections;

(b) physically capable of being moved from one place to another by road (whether by being towed, or by being transported on a motor vehicle or trailer). For the purpose of this section a caravan is deemed to be physically capable of being moved even where it would not be lawful to move it when fully assembled;[18]

(c) not in excess of any of the following dimensions:

   (i)   length (exclusive of any drawbar), 60 feet;

   (ii) width, 20 feet;

   (iii) overall height of living accommodation (measured internally from the floor at the lowest level to the ceiling at the highest level), 10 feet.[19]

Definition of "Caravan Site"

The statutory definition is contained in section 1(4) of the Act. By virtue of that section, a caravan site is expressed to mean:

   "... land on which a caravan is stationed for the

---

[16] *Taylor v. Calvert* [1978] 2 All E.R. 630 (per Lord Denning M.R.).
[17] 1968 Act, s. 13(1).
[18] For road traffic restrictions, see ch. 16.
[19] Equivalent measurements in metres are: length 18.288; width 6.096; overall height 3.048.

purposes of human habitation and land which is used in conjunction with land on which a caravan is so stationed."

Many people will find it surprising that a caravan in their garden could constitute a caravan site for which a site licence is required. In practice, however, the parking and use of a caravan within the curtilage of a home does not usually require a site licence or planning permission so long as it is merely being used for a purpose incidental to the enjoyment of the home.[20] This will be so if, for example, (as is often the case) the caravan is used for additional sleeping or living accommodation by members of the household who continue to use the home. It would not, presumably, extend to a letting on a commercial basis.

The case law on this subject may conveniently be analysed by dividing the section into three naturally distinct parts.

(1) "Land on which a caravan is stationed"
It is clear that these words are intended to refer to the land itself and not to the caravans on it. A site is not to be defined, for example, by fixing the date on which caravans had to be stationed on the land.[21] Nor is the definition applicable to the number of caravans so stationed, as is apparent from the decision in *Minister of Housing and Local Government v. Hartnell.*[22]

In that case a site owner had, for over four years prior to the passing of the Act, kept up to six caravans on the northern section of his field. He was granted a site licence by the local authority subject to the conditions that no more than six caravans should be stationed on the site, and that no caravan should be moved onto any other part of his field. It was held, by the House of Lords, that these

---

[20] See p. 53.
[21] *Biss v. Smallburgh R.D.C.* (1964) 15 P. & C.R. 351.
[22] (1965) 1 All E.R. 490, H.L.

conditions were *ultra vires*. In the course of his judgment, Lord Wilberforce made reference to the above distinction. He said:

> "To say that one cannot have an existing site unless there is both a piece of land and a number of caravans on it is not the same thing as to say that the number of caravans in fact there enters into the definition of an existing site."

There may, indeed, be some instances where it is not necessary for a caravan to be physically stationed on land at all for such land to be a site within the meaning of the Act. Both Lord Justice Harman and the Lord Justice Davies, in the case of *Biss v. Smallburgh R.D.C.*,[23] considered that if caravans were temporarily absent owing to the season of the year, or perhaps for other reasons such as decoration or repair, the land on which they had been stationed would still be in use as a caravan site. It must be doubted, however, whether land which was merely being prepared for use would come within the definition.

In *Roy Crimble Ltd. v. Edgecombe*,[24] it was held that a houseboat which is moored to the verge of a protected site is not a caravan stationed on a caravan site within the meaning of section 1(4) of the 1960 Act.

(2) "For the purposes of human habitation"
It is only sites that are used for the purpose of human habitation that come within the purview of the Act. In *Devon County Council v. Horton*,[25] it was held that sites on which caravans were merely being stored fell outside the Act. So too, it would seem, would sites on which caravans were being displayed or harboured.

In this respect there is also the situation contemplated in the above-mentioned case of *Biss v. Smallburgh R.D.C.*

---

[23] p. 23.
[24] (1981) 131 N.L.J. 928, C.A.
[25] (1962) 61 L.G.R. 60.

Lord Justice Harman there said that:

> "The word 'site' connotes a place habitually devoted to some purpose and caravans are not 'stationed' for the purposes of section 1(4) of the 1960 Act, on an area where one or two of them has or have casually stopped for a night or more even though other caravans may have stopped in the vicinity for several years."[26]

(3) "Land which is used in conjunction"

Although the extent of land used "in conjunction" with land on which a caravan is stationed is, essentially, a question of fact and degree, the cases of *Williams-Denton v. Watford R.D.C.*[27] and *R. v. Axbridge R.D.C. ex parte Wormald*[28] seems to show that it is only a very limited area that acquires rights.

In *Wormald's Case* the applicant owned some two and a half acres of land. On the land stood a bungalow and a caravan. He was issued with a site licence only in respect of the small piece of land on which the caravan stood, and a radius of about twenty feet. He claimed to be entitled to a site licence for the whole two and a half acres.

The Court of Appeal rejected the claim. In so doing, Lord Denning M.R. gave some illustrations of the meaning of the above phrase. He said:

> "... land for a latrine or on which a motor car stands, or land laid out as a playground, would be part of the site; but not waste land over which children or adults may run from time to time."

Definition of "Occupier"

The word "occupier" is not altogether straightforward in that it has a different meaning under the provisions

---

[26] *Cf.* First Sch., para. 2 of the 1960 Act and ch. 5.
[27] (1963) 15 P. & C.R. 11.
[28] (1964) 1 All E.R. 571.

relating to caravan control from that under subsequent legislation in respect of caravans.[29]

For the purpose of the 1960 Act an occupier means, under section 1(3) thereof:

> "... in relation to any land, the person who, by virtue of an estate or interest therein held by him, is entitled to possession thereof or would be so entitled but for the rights of any other person under any licence granted in respect of the land."

Where, however, land which does not exceed four hundred square yards in area is *let* under a tenancy entered into with a view to the use of the land as a caravan site then, in relation to that land, the occupier is the person who would be entitled to possession but for the rights of any person under that tenancy.

The distinction to be borne in mind is between the licensor and the lessor. The licensor is always liable for causing or permitting land to be used as a caravan site without a site licence. The lessor will only be liable if the land is less than four hundred square yards in area and if the tenancy was entered into with a view to the use of the land as a caravan site.

The effect of this distinction is that a site operator who lets off small pitches on a site for individual caravans will remain the occupier but, where he lets a larger area under a tenancy for use as a caravan site, then the tenant will be the occupier.

Section 12 of the Act gives the occupier powers to ensure that his tenant or licensee (as defined in section 1(3) of the Act) complies with the terms of a site licence.

In particular, section 12(1) makes it a condition of any such licence or tenancy that, if any person in exercise of

---

[29] *Cf.* the 1968 and 1983 Acts; see ch. 9.

rights under the licence or tenancy does anything which would constitute an offence under section 1 if he were the occupier[30] of the land, then the person who is the occupier thereof may take possession of the land and terminate the licence or tenancy.

---

[30] i.e. causing or permitting the land to be used as a caravan site without a site licence.

Chapter 4

THE GRANT OF PLANNING PERMISSION

General Planning Control

Subject to certain exceptions, which will be considered later, planning permission is required for the carrying out of any development of land.[1]

"Development" is defined in section 55 of the Town and Country Planning Act 1990 to mean the carrying out of building, engineering, mining or other operations in, on, over or under land, or the making of any material change in the use of any buildings or other land. In relation to caravans, it is this latter aspect of a material change of use that is most important and that gives rise to the most problems.

Under the system of caravan control introduced by the 1960 Act, however, planning permission is necessary before a site licence may be granted. Even after a site licence has been obtained, planning problems may arise. An increase in the number of caravans on site, for example, may amount to a material change of use and necessitate a further application for planning permission. It is, therefore, essential for those concerned with caravans and sites to have a basic knowledge of planning law.

Form of Application and Certification

Application for planning permission should be made, where land is outside Greater London, to the local planning authority (normally the district or unitary council). If the land is in Greater London, the application should be lodged with the council of the London borough in which the land is situated, or with the Common Council as the case may be.

---

[1]   Town and Country Planning Act 1990, s. 57.

In general, the planning authority will give their decision within two months. It is, however, possible to extend this period by written agreement between the applicant and the authority.[2]

In order to prevent owners or agricultural tenants being unaware of proposals to develop their land, no application for planning permission may be entertained unless it is accompanied by one of four certificates stating, essentially, that the requisite notice has been given or that, in the circumstances, it is unnecessary to give such notice.

Publicity for Applications

The local planning authority must publicise applications for certain types of major development. The only one which might be relevant to caravan sites is development carried out on a site having an area of one hectare or more.[3]

Other Forms of Application

There are two further types of application that an applicant may wish to make.

(1) Outline Planning Permission

This is an enquiry to find out how the planning authority would view a proposed type of development, and what conditions are likely to be imposed. It should be noted, however, that the procedure is restricted to development involving the erection of a building.

From the point of view of an applicant who wants to develop land as a caravan site, an application for outline permission has two main advantages. It avoids the need to provide detailed plans, in the first instance, dealing with such matters as sanitary blocks, water points, etc. Also, where the applicant does not own the land in question, the

---

[2]   T.C.P. (General Development Procedure) Order 1995, art. 20.
[3]   T.C.P. (General Permitted Development) Order 1995, art. 12.

procedure enables him to ascertain whether planning permission is going to be granted before entering into a purchase of the land.

Assuming that outline planning permission is granted, the applicant is required to make a further application for approval of "reserved matters".[4] These relate to details not provided in the outline application and which concern the siting, design or external appearance of the building, or the means of access, or the landscaping of the site.

An application for outline planning permission and for the approval of reserved matters will be determined within the same period as for an application for ordinary planning permission.[5]

(2) Application to Determine if Planning Permission is Required
Although planning permission will usually be required in the case of caravan sites, there may be instances where an applicant is unsure whether an application is necessary. This may be so where, for example, it is uncertain whether the use of caravans on land falls within the category of permitted development and outside the scheme of the 1960 Act.[6] It may also be so where the "development" occurs after the grant of the site licence.[7]

It is, accordingly, provided by section 192 of the 1990 Act that a person who proposes to carry out any operations on land, or to make any change in the use of land, may apply to the local planning authority for a determination as to whether or not the operations or change would be lawful.

Duration of Planning Permission
There are various provisions in the 1990 Act designed to ensure that development is undertaken within a reasonable

---

[4]   1990 Act, s. 92 and T.C.P. (General Development Procedure) Order 1995, art. 4.
[5]   See p. 27.
[6]   See p. 53.
[7]   As in the case of an increase in the number of caravans on site.

period. In the context of caravan law, the reason for these rules is clear. Much uncertainty would be created in local planning policy if developers, who had obtained planning permission, were allowed to take up that permission at any time. Caravan sites might remain unused for years, and later applications for development would be likely to be refused because of the planning authority's fear of sudden development.

By virtue of section 91(1) of the 1990 Act, most planning permissions are granted subject to the condition that development must be begun within five years from the date of the grant. The position is otherwise where the planning authority specify a different period, or where the permission is granted for a limited period.[8]

In the case of applications for outline permission, the development must be begun not later than whichever is the later of: (a) five years from the grant of outline permission, or (b) two years from final approval of the reserved matters.[9]

Where development is begun but not completed within a required period, the planning authority may serve a completion notice which has the effect of terminating a planning permission after a further period of at least twelve months.[10]

Revocation and Modification of Planning Permission

Planning permission for a caravan site is valuable and should be utilised quickly. In clear cases of delay, completion notices will be served and the permission will, on expiration of the notices, cease to be valid.

There may, however, be other instances where the provisions as to duration are not necessarily infringed but

---

[8]   1990 Act, s. 91(1).
[9]   1990 Act, s. 92(2).
[10]   1990 Act, s. 94.

where development is not undertaken immediately and there are strong reasons for preventing it from being undertake or continued. In certain cases, there is power under the 1990 Act to revoke or modify a permission.

Section 97(1) of the 1990 Act provides that the planning authority may, where they consider it expedient to do so, by order revoke or modify a permission to such extent as they consider expedient. Before doing so they must have regard to: (i) the development plan, and (ii) any other material considerations.

The power is not intended to apply to development already carried out.[11] Unless there is no objection to an order of revocation or modification being made, such an order is not valid unless confirmed by the Secretary of State.[12]

Orders Requiring Discontinuance of Use or Alteration or Removal of Buildings or Works

The planning authority may, in certain circumstances, make an order requiring development that has already been carried out to be discontinued, or altered or removed. The purpose of this is to prevent development, even though lawfully in existence, from conflicting with current planning requirements.

There are several situations in which such an order might be made in respect of a caravan site. The area in which the site is situated may have completely changed in character since planning permission was first granted as, for example, by reason of a heavy increase in residential development. Another instance might occur where there was now a need for recreational facilities rather than a permanent residential site in the area.

By virtue of section 102 of the 1990 Act, where the

---

[11]   1990 Act, s. 97(4).
[12]   1990 Act, ss. 98 and 99.

planning authority consider it expedient in the interests of proper planning of their area, including the interests of amenity, they may make an order:

(i) that any use of land should be discontinued or that any conditions should be imposed on the continuance of a use of land; or

(ii) that any buildings or works should be altered or removed.

Before making such an order, the authority must have regard to the development plan and to any other material considerations. As in the case of revocation or modification, an order under section 102 requires confirmation by the Secretary of State.[13]

The power to order discontinuance, etc. is clearly a drastic one. It may cause considerable hardship to caravan dwellers who have lived for years on a site that has been lawfully developed. Section 102(6) of the 1990 Act therefore imposes a duty on the planning authority (in the event of displacement), to provide alternative accommodation if there is none reasonably available. There is also provision, under section 115, for the payment of compensation in certain circumstances.

There are various prescribed penalties for failure to comply with an order under section 102.[14] In addition, section 189(2) provides that, where an order requires an alteration or removal of buildings and works, and it is not complied with, the planning authority may (and shall if required by direction of the Secretary of State), enter onto the land and take such steps as are specified in the confirmed order.

---

[13] 1990 Act, s. 103.
[14] 1990 Act, s. 189, i.e. a fine of £5,000 on summary conviction and £50 per day if non-compliance continues. On indictment the extent of the fines is unlimited.

Criteria for Consideration of Planning Permission

Section 55A of the 1990 Act requires the planning authority to determine an application in accordance with the development plan, unless material considerations indicate otherwise. Section 70(1) provides that the authority, in determining an application for planning permission, must have regard to: (i) the provisions of the development plan, so far as material,[15] and (ii) to any other material consideration. Having done so they may either grant planning permission unconditionally, or subject to such conditions as they think fit, or refuse it.

It is difficult to specify what may or may not amount to a "material consideration" in each particular case; clearly this is a matter very much within the authority's own province. For example, in *Rhodes v. Minister of Housing and Local Government,*[16] it was held that the availability of an alternative caravan site may be a factor to be taken into account, but that it would depend on the nature of the application in each case.

In general terms, although material considerations must be of a planning nature, they are not limited to questions of amenity. Any consideration is relevant that concerns private or public interest relating to the use and development of land.[17] In *Wells v. Minister of Housing and Local Government,*[18] the fact that planning permission had already been granted was held to be a material consideration for the purpose of a subsequent application.

Conditions Attached to Planning Permission

As has been seen, the planning authority may grant planning permission "subject to such conditions as they think fit". It might be thought that the authority have unlimited power to impose any conditions, however

---

[15]   See P.P.G. 1 (paras. 50-56).
[16]   [1963] 1 W.L.R. 208; (1963) 14 P. & C.R. 122.
[17]   *Stringer v. Minister of Housing and Local Government* [1971] 1 All E.R. 65.
[18]   [1967] 1 W.L.R. 1000; (1967) 18 P. & C.R. 401.

restrictive. In fact, it is apparent that this is not the case and that the conditions attached to a permission must be appropriate from a planning viewpoint.

In the leading case of *Pyx Granite Co. Ltd. v. Ministry of Housing and Local Government*,[19] Lord Denning M.R., in reviewing the scope of certain planning conditions, stated as a general principle that:

> "... the law says that those conditions, to be valid, must fairly and reasonably relate to the permitted development. The planning authority are not at liberty to use their powers for an ulterior object, however desirable that object may seem to be in the public interest."

The later case of *Chertsey U.D.C. v. Mixnam's Properties Ltd.*[20] was concerned with conditions attached to a caravan site licence rather than those under a planning permission. Nevertheless, in the course of an important judgment in the Court of Appeal, Willmer L.J. laid down certain general principles relating to the imposition of conditions under a statutory power.[21]

Planning Policy Towards Caravan Sites

There is no specific government planning policy on caravan sites, save that in Annex B to P.P.G. 21 on Tourism (1992 edition). Annex B covers the use of land for holiday and touring caravan sites.

Appeal Against Planning Refusal or Conditions

There is provision under various sections of the 1990 Act for appeals to be made on notice to the Secretary of State in respect of certain matters.

---

[19]   [1958] 1 Q.B. 554, C.A. The decision was reversed on other grounds in the House of Lords, *cf.* [1959] 3 All E.R. 1, H.L.

[20]   [1964] 2 All E.R. 627.

[21]   See ch. 5.

A right of appeal lies in the following circumstances, namely:

(1) Where an application is made to a planning authority for planning permission, or for approval of matters reserved in an outline planning permission, and that permission or approval is refused, or else granted subject to conditions which are disputed (s. 78(1)).

(2) Where the planning authority have not given notice of their decision, or notice that the application has been referred to the Secretary of State (s. 78(2)).

(3) Where the planning authority have refused a certificate of lawful use under section 192 of the 1990 Act (s. 195(1)).[22]

The rules as to appeal are, briefly, as follows:

(1) Notice of appeal must be given to the Secretary of State within six months of the decision (or failure to give notice) appealed against, or such longer period as the Secretary of State may allow[23] (T.C.P. (General Development Procedure) Order 1995, art. 23(1)).

(2) A copy of certain documents must be sent to the Secretary of State. These include a copy of the application itself, notice of the decision or determination (if any), and all relevant plans, drawings, particulars and documents connected with the application (*ibid.*, art 23(3)).

(3) Every appeal must be accompanied by one of four certificates issued pursuant to art. 6 (*ibid.*, art 7).

(4) Before determining an appeal, the Secretary of State must, if either the applicant or the planning authority so desire, afford to each an opportunity of being

---

[22] See p. 28.
[23] Notices of appeal may be obtained on application to the Secretary of State.

heard by a person appointed by the Secretary of State for the purpose (s. 79(2)).

By virtue of section 79(1) of the 1990 Act, the Secretary of State has power to allow or dismiss the appeal, or to reverse or vary any part of the planning authority's decision whether the appeal relates to that part or not. He may deal with the application as if it had been made to him in the first instance.

The decision of the Secretary of State is final so far as appeals are concerned.[24] In certain limited instances, however, it is possible to question the validity of such a decision on the rather narrow ground that the determination is not within the powers of the 1990 Act, or that any of the relevant requirements have not been complied with. Application must be made to the High Court within six weeks of the decision, and may be made by either the planning authority or applicant to the original appeal.[25] In practice, appeals against the Secretary of State's determination are not likely to be frequent.

Exemption from the Requirement of Planning Permission

In the context of caravan law, planning permission is not required for certain specified uses (described on pages 53-56 below) which correspond to the exceptions from the general requirement of a site licence. These are the exceptions contained in Schedule 1 to the Caravan Sites and Control of Development Act 1960 (other than those relating to winter quarters), specified in paragraph 10 of that Schedule.[26]

The conditions or permission not being required are that the use shall be discontinued when the circumstances in each case cease to exist, and that then all caravans on the site should be removed.[27]

---

[24] 1990 Act, s. 284.
[25] 1990 Act, ss. 288 and 289.
[26] See ch. 5, p. 56.
[27] T. & C.P. (General Permitted Development) Order 1995, art. 3.

Apart from the above exemptions, planning permission is not required for development that may be required under the conditions of a current site licence.[28]

Consultation Between Local Authorities

By virtue of section 71(3) of the 1990 Act, where an application is made for planning permission as a preliminary to obtaining a site licence, the planning authority must, unless they are also the site licensing authority for the land in question, consult the local authority who have the power to issue the site licence before granting that permission.

The obligation relates only to consultation. There is no requirement of agreement between the two authorities. However, the opinion of the site licensing authority may well have a bearing on the nature of the permission that is finally granted.

---

[28]   1995 Order, Sch. 1, Part 5, Classes A and B.

Chapter 5

THE GRANT OF THE SITE LICENCE

Form of Application

Where a site licence is required, application should be made by the occupier[1] to the local authority in whose area the land is situated.[2]

There is no specified form of application as in the case of planning permission. It is, however, necessary that the application should be in writing and that it specifies the land in question.[3]

Either at the time of making the application or subsequently, it is necessary to supply the local authority with certain particulars.

The required particulars are contained in the Schedule to the Caravan Sites (Licence Applications) Order 1960.[4] Apart from administrative details, the most important particulars set out in the Order are these:

(1) The type of caravan site for which the licence is required, that is: permanent, residential, seasonal or touring.

(2) The maximum number of caravans that are proposed to be stationed on site at any one time for the purpose of human habitation.

(3) A layout plan of the site, to a scale of not less than 1/500, showing the boundaries of the site, the positions of caravan standings and, where appropriate, the

---

[1]   As defined in s. 1(3) of the 1960 Act; see ch. 3.
[2]   1960 Act, s. 3(1).
[3]   1960 Act, s. 3(2). A suitable form is obtainable from Shaw & Sons, Cat. No. M50C.
[4]   S.I. 1960 No. 1474.

positions of roads and footpaths, toilet blocks, stores and other buildings, foul and surface water drainage, water supply, recreation spaces, fire points and parking spaces.

(4) Details of the arrangements for refuse disposal and for sewage and waste water disposal.

It will be seen that the application for a site licence is considerably easier than the corresponding one for planning permission. As has been stated, the site licence is, ordinarily, issued automatically on application once planning permission has been obtained. The purpose of the requirement of particulars is so that the local authority can determine what conditions ought to be attached to the site licence. The application itself is treated as complete before the particulars are given.

Issuing the Site Licence

Subject to one important exception, the local authority are directed to issue a site licence to an applicant who is entitled to planning permission and who has furnished the prescribed particulars.

Where the applicant already has planning permission when he provides the particulars, the local authority must issue the licence within two months of the particulars being given. If planning permission is not obtained until later, the licence must be issued within six weeks of the permission being obtained. In each case the period may be extended by written agreement between the applicant and the local authority.[5] This may be desirable where, for example, negotiations are in progress over conditions and it is not wished to prejudice those negotiations by the premature issue of a licence.

In computing the respective periods within which the licence must be issued, the days on which the particulars

---

[5] 1960 Act, s. 3(4) and (5).

were provided or the planning permission was obtained should not be included.[6]

The consequence of failing to issue a site licence as directed is that no offence of causing or permitting land to be used as a caravan site, under section 1(1) of the 1960 Act, is committed by the applicant. This remains the case until a site licence is issued.[7] However, the fact that a licence is issued outside the prescribed period does not render it invalid, nor does it fetter the powers of the local authority in respect of the conditions that may be attached to it.[8]

There is one instance in which a site licence must not be issued even where an applicant may have obtained planning permission and has submitted particulars. It is provided by section 3(6) of the 1960 Act that no licence may be issued to a person who has, to the knowledge of the local authority, held a site licence which has been revoked less than three years before.[9]

In one respect, the section would appear to be unfortunately phrased. The statutory restriction operates in the case of a person who has held a licence which has been revoked. It would presumably be possible, therefore, for a site owner to transfer his interest to another person who later had the licence revoked. If the original site owner wished to apply for a new site licence within three years of the revocation he would, on the literal meaning of the section 3(6), be prevented from doing so even though he had done nothing to bring about the revocation.

Duration of the Site Licence

Although, as will be seen, the local authority have wide powers to impose conditions, they are not permitted to

---

[6] *Stewart v. Chapman* [1951] 2 K.B. 792.
[7] 1960 Act, s. 6.
[8] *Rees v. James* (1963) 61 L.G.R. 318.
[9] See ch. 6.

issue a site licence for a limited period unless the relevant planning permission is stated to be for a limited period. Where that is the case, the site licence must be stated to expire at the same time as the planning permission.[10]

It is provided by section 29(3) of the 1960 Act that planning permission granted for the use of the land for intermittent periods is not to be regarded as expiring at any time so long as the permission authorises the use of the land for further intermittent periods.

If, after the site licence has been issued, the terms of the planning permission are varied on appeal, the licence must be altered by the local authority who issued it so as to ensure that the length of the licence and planning permission are the same.[11] In order to make the necessary alterations, the local authority may require the licence holder to deliver up the licence to them. If he fails to do so, without reasonable excuse, there is a penalty, on summary conviction, of a maximum fine of Level 1 on the standard scale (currently £200).[12]

Transfer and Transmission of the Site Licence

The only way in which a site licence may be transferred is from one occupier to another. The term "occupier" is a technical one and its meaning has already been discussed.[13] By virtue of section 10(1) of the 1960 Act, where the holder of a site licence ceases to be the occupier of the land he may, with the consent of the local authority in whose area the land is situated, transfer the licence to the person who then becomes the occupier of the land.

If the local authority approve the transfer, they must endorse on the licence the name of the person to whom it is to be transferred, and the date agreed between the

---

[10]   1960 Act, s. 4(1).
[11]   1960 Act, s. 4(2).
[12]   1960 Act, s. 11(1) and (2) (as amended).
[13]   See ch. 3.

parties for that person to become the licence holder.[14]

Although the local authority may refuse to consent to a transfer, there seems little practical point in their doing so. A proposed transferee is empowered to make application himself for a site licence, provided that an application has also been made for the authority to give their consent to a transfer. If consent is given, it is not necessary to proceed with the application for a site licence. However, if consent is not forthcoming, the transferee must be issued with a site licence in compliance with his application.[15]

There are, however, several minor advantages in requiring the authority's consent – even as a formality. These include:

(1) By withholding consent, the authority can force a transferee to seek a new site licence. They can take the opportunity – if they deem it appropriate – of altering the conditions on the new licence.

(2) The system of referring transfers to the authority ensures that all transfers are properly registered. This makes it all the easier to check, for example, whether a transferee has had a site licence revoked within the previous three years.

There is also provision in the 1960 Act relating to the transmission of a site licence. Under section 10(4) thereof, a person who becomes an occupier, by operation of law, becomes the new licence holder from the date that his occupation commences. Upon his application, the local authority are directed to endorse his name and date of his occupation on the site licence. The section covers such persons as the personal representative or the trustee in bankruptcy on the death or bankruptcy of the original licence holder.

---

[14]   1960 Act, s. 10(2).
[15]   1960 Act, s. 10(3).

Every local authority must keep a register of site licences in respect of land in their area. Such registers must be available for public inspection at all reasonable times. Where, on transfer or transmission, names and dates have been endorsed on a site licence, the same details should be recorded on the register.[16]

Imposing Conditions on the Site Licence

The most important aspect of site licences is the nature and extent of the conditions that may be imposed. As applicants are, in general, entitled to be issued with a site licence once they have obtained planning permission, it is only through the imposition of conditions that the local authority are able to exert an effective measure of control. From the point of view of both sides, it is important to know how far that control is able to be exercised.

Section 5(1) of the 1960 Act lays down the general power to attach conditions and then, without prejudice to that power, gives specific types of conditions that may be imposed.

So far as the general power is concerned, it is provided that the local authority may impose such conditions as they think "necessary and desirable" in the interests of one or more of three categories of persons, namely:

(1) Persons dwelling on the land in caravans.

(2) Any other class of persons.

(3) The public at large.

Although the local authority would appear to have an almost unlimited discretion in the matter, a body of case law has built up which effectively circumscribes that discretion.

The leading case on the nature and extent of site licence conditions is the decision in *Chertsey U.D.C. v. Mixnam's*

---

[16]   1960 Act, s. 25(1) and (2).

Properties.[17] Although the case went to the House of Lords, which affirmed the decision of the Court of Appeal, it was in the Court of Appeal that Willmer L.J. laid down, in an important judgment, the principles relating to the imposition of conditions under a statutory power.

In the opinion of Willmer L.J., the statutory power to impose conditions, however widely expressed, was subject to four distinct qualifications. They are:

(1) The conditions must not be such as to effect a fundamental alteration in the general law relating to the rights of the persons on whom they are imposed, unless the power to effect such an alteration is expressed in the clearest possible terms.

(2) The power to impose conditions must be limited by reference to the subject matter of the statute.

(3) The conditions must not be unreasonable such as Parliament cannot have intended to impose. In this respect there is an analogy with a power to make byelaws which would be regarded as unreasonable and *ultra vires* if:

   (i)   they were found to be partial and unequal in their operation as between different classes;

   (ii) they were manifestly unjust;

   (iii) they disclosed bad faith;

   (iv) they involved such oppressive or gratuitous interference with the rights of those subject to them as could find not justification in the minds of reasonable men.

(4) A condition may be held void for uncertainty and unenforceable if it is ambiguous or uncertain in its application.

---

[17]   [1964] 2 All E.R. 267; 15 P. & C.R. 331. The Court of Appeal judgment is at [1963] 3 W.L.R. 38.

In applying those general considerations to the facts of the case, the Court of Appeal held to be void a number of conditions imposed under a site licence by Chertsey U.D.C.

The council had attached conditions providing that site rents must first be agreed with them, and that security of tenure – similar to that under the then Rent Acts (now largely repealed or spent) – must be granted to all caravan dwellers. There were also conditions restricting the kind of site rules that the occupier could draw up. The council wanted the rules to extend only to those items normally covered by a tenancy agreement, and not to place any restrictions as to from whom commodities could be purchased or as to the formation of a tenants' association.

Both Danckwerts L.J. and Diplock L.J. stressed, in their respective judgments, that conditions under a site licence should be restricted to the physical conditions of the licensed site. What Chertsey U.D.C. were attempting to do was to govern the contractual relationship between the site owner and caravan dwellers which was contrary to the intention of the 1960 Act. In his judgment, Danckwerts L.J. stated that conditions should be aimed at securing:

> "the provision of proper facilities in respect of sanitation and amenities so that the site should not become a menace to the health of the occupants of the caravans or other persons who might be affected by the site, and also to prevent the site becoming an eyesore, or in any other way a nuisance to the members of the public who may dwell in the neighbourhood or pass through the locality."

It is not altogether easy to determine what attitude the courts might adopt to novel kinds of conditions. In practice, however, the discretion of the local authority is still probably fairly wide.

Conditions requiring a site to be "kept free of unauthorised tents and structures"[18] and limiting the number of caravans[19] have both been upheld. A condition designed to preserve the visual amenity of a site for the benefit of the public by requiring the removal of caravans from the site in winter was held to be a planning matter and could not be validly imposed as a site licence condition.[20] It is, however, statutorily provided that no condition may be attached to a licence which controls the type of caravans to be stationed upon the site by reference to the materials used in their construction.[21]

One important limitation that does exist on the powers of the authority is provided by the connection between planning and site licence control. It is clearly established that, in imposing conditions under a site licence, the local authority are not permitted to go beyond the limits of the planning permission.

This is well illustrated by the decision in *R. v. Kent Justices ex parte Crittenden*.[22] In that case, the planning authority had granted planning permission for land to be used as a caravan site subject to the condition that the number of caravans on site should not exceed thirteen. Subsequently, the local authority issued a site licence subject to the same condition. The justices, on an appeal against the condition, refused to make any order stating that they had no jurisdiction to consider the matter in view of the terms of the planning permission. They were upheld by the Divisional Court, on an application by the site owner for an order of *mandamus*, on the basis that the grant of a site licence under section 3(3) of the 1960 Act must be confined to the limits of the planning permission including any conditions attached to it.

---

18 *Carnall v. Jones* (1966) 18 P. & C.R. 436, D.C.
19 *Esdell Caravan Parks Ltd. v. Hemel Hempstead R.D.C.* [1965] 3 All E.R. 737.
20 *Babbage v. North Norfolk D.C.* [1990] 1 P.L.R. 65.
21 1960 Act, s. 5(2).
22 [1963] 2 All E.R. 245; 14 P. & C.R. 456; 61 L.G.R. 346.

The point was put succinctly by Lord Parker C.J. when he said:

> "To have two controls covering in any respect the same ground, and to permit the added and later control to enlarge the user while the original and earlier control still remains in force seems quite unreal ... To take an example, can it really be said that the scheme of legislation permits the local authority to impose a condition that the caravans be painted red when the planning permission has provided that they shall be green?"

Particular Conditions

Although the local authority have a general power to impose conditions, section 5(1) of the 1960 Act lays down certain specific conditions – in the nature of a guide – that may be imposed. These may be summarised as follows:

(1) For restricting the occasions on which caravans are to be stationed, or the total number of caravans to be stationed at any time.

(2) For controlling the types of caravans on site.

(3) For regulating the positions in which caravans are to be stationed, and for regulating or prohibiting the placing of structures, vehicles and tents on the land.

(4) For ensuring that amenities are preserved including the planting and replanting with trees and bushes.

(5) For securing that proper measures are taken for the prevention and detection of fire, and that adequate means of fighting fire are provided and maintained.

(6) For securing and maintaining adequate sanitary and other facilities, services and equipment.

In addition, there is one condition which the local authority are directed to impose unless the site is restricted to three caravans or less. It is that a copy of the site licence should be displayed on the site in a conspicuous place.[23] The purpose of this is to give the occupants of the caravans an opportunity of making themselves acquainted with the conditions under which the site licence has been granted.

If a condition under a site licence requires the carrying out of works on the land, the local authority may also prohibit or restrict the bringing of caravans on to the land until they certify in writing that the works have been completed to their satisfaction. They may also set a time limit for the completion of the works where the land is, at the time, in use as a caravan site.[24] Moreover, a condition requiring works to be carried out is not invalidated merely because the site licence holder is not entitled, as of right, to carry out the works.[25]

Model Standards

Section 5(6) of the 1960 Act provides that model standards may be specified by the Secretary of State with regard to the layout of caravan sites or particular types of caravan site, and the provision of facilities, services and equipment for such sites. The local authority are directed to have regard to these standards when deciding what (if any) conditions to attach to the site licence.

Model standards have been published.[26] They deal with a number of matters, the most important of which relate to:

(1) Density of, and space between, caravans.

(2) Good roads and footpaths being provided on site.

---

[23] 1960 Act, s. 5(3).
[24] 1960 Act, s. 5(4).
[25] 1960 Act, s. 5(5). Planning permission for development required by the conditions of a site licence is, subject to standard conditions, given by the T.C.P. (General Permitted Development) Order 1995, art. 3, Sch. 1, Part 5, Classes A and B.
[26] Reproduced in Appendix A, p. 163.

(3) Adequate sanitation and refuse disposal.

(4) Adequate storage, car parking and recreational space.

These standards are, however, by no means binding.[27] They should not be applied rigidly. In particular, a local authority should consider what are the minimum, rather than the maximum, conditions to be imposed. The standards are intended to apply only to permanent residential caravan sites, to static holiday caravan sites and to sites on which there are both static and touring caravans but where the predominant use is for static holiday caravans.

Separate model standards for holiday caravan sites were published by the Development of the Environment in 1983 under cover of Circular 23/83, and these are reproduced in Appendix B, page 173.

Appeal Against Conditions
A right of appeal against conditions attached to a site licence is afforded by section 7(1) of the Act. It is apparent, from the wording of the section, that this right is restricted to the site licence holder and that it does not extend, for example, to a caravan dweller or to another site owner.

The section provides that any person aggrieved by any condition, subject to which a site licence has been issued to him, may appeal to a magistrates' court acting for the petty sessions area in which the land is situated, within twenty-eight days of the licence being issued. The one exception to this is that there is no right of appeal against the mandatory condition requiring display of the licence on site.

If the condition that is being appealed against is one requiring the carrying out of works on the land, that condition, by virtue of section 7(2), has no effect for

---

[27]   *Clyde Caravans (Longbank) Ltd. v. Renfrew C.C.* [1962] S.L.T. 20.

twenty-eight days thereafter or, if an appeal has been entered, while such an appeal is pending.

The form of appeal is by way of complaint for an order.[28] In computing the time limit for appealing, the day on which the licence was issued should not be included.[29] The time limit is, however, strict and there is no statutory provision for extending it.[30] There is no further right of appeal from a magistrates' court unless a point of law is involved. In such a case, the correct procedure is to ask the justices to state a case and to apply by way of case stated to the Divisional Court.

In deciding an appeal, the court must be satisfied that the condition being appealed against is, in the words of section 7(1), "unduly burdensome". If so satisfied, there is a discretion to vary or cancel it. It does not, however, automatically follow that the condition will be interfered with.[31] The onus of establishing that a particular condition is unduly burdensome lies on the appellant but it is up to the justices to decide whether the burden of the condition outweighs its benefit to the public.[32]

There are few precise criteria for determining whether a condition is unduly burdensome. The court is, by section 7(1), directed to have regard to any model standards. However, as has been indicated, these standards are not binding. In particular, a condition may be unduly burdensome even where it conforms to model standards.[33]

In *Esdell Caravan Parks Ltd. v. Hemel Hempstead R.D.C.*,[34] it was held by the Court of Appeal that relevant factors for

---

[28] See the Magistrates' Courts Rules 1981, S.I. 1981 No. 552 (as amended).
[29] *Stewart v. Chapman* [1951] 2 K.B. 792.
[30] It may, however, be possible to apply for an alteration of conditions; see p. 50.
[31] *Llanfyllin R.D.C. v. Holland* (1964) 62 L.G.R. 459, D.C.
[32] *Owen Cooper Estates v. Lexden and Winstree R.D.C.* (1964) 16 P. & C.R. 233.
[33] *United British Caravan Company v. Dunbarton C.C.* [1962] S.L.T. 37.
[34] [1965] 3 All E.R. 737.

determining whether a condition is burdensome include considerations such as public health, education, transport facilities and the social balance between villagers and caravan dwellers. Purely planning considerations are not relevant because they will already have been taken into account by the planning authority when deciding whether to grant planning permission. There is, moreover, a different system of appeal in respect of conditions attached to a planning permission.

There may, of course, be occasions where site licence and planning conditions overlap. Where, for example, the site licence authority impose a severe restriction on numbers so as to prevent planning permission from becoming effective, there could be no objection to an appeal being presented on the ground that the condition was unduly burdensome.

Alteration of Conditions

Conditions attached to a site licence are not necessarily permanent. Section 8(1) of the Act states that the local authority may, at any time, alter such conditions by varying or cancelling them, by adding new conditions, or by a combination of these methods. Before doing so, the authority are obliged to afford to the licence holder an opportunity of making representations. No alteration, moreover, becomes effective unless and until written notification thereof has been received by the licence holder.[35]

Where the local authority decide to exercise their powers under section 8(1), they may require the licence holder to deliver up the licence for the purpose of making the requisite alterations. If he fails to do so, without reasonable excuse, there is a penalty, on summary conviction, of a maximum fine of Level 1 on the standard scale (currently £250).[36]

---

[35]   1960 Act, s. 8(3).
[36]   1960 Act, s. 11(1) and (2) (as amended).

A right of appeal, similar to that available on the imposition of conditions, is given by section 8(2) of the Act. It is there provided that, where a site licence holder is aggrieved by either: (i) any alteration of conditions, or (ii) the refusal of the local authority of an application by him for the alteration of conditions, he may – within twenty-eight days of receiving written notification of the decision – appeal to a magistrates' court acting for the petty sessions area in which the land is situated. If the court allow the appeal, they are empowered to give the local authority such directions as may be necessary to give effect to their decision.

It should be observed that, as with similar provisions, the day on which notification is received is not included in computing the time allowed for appeal.[37]

Where the local authority alter a condition so as to require a licence holder to carry out works on the land, such alteration, by virtue of section 8(3), has no effect for twenty-eight days thereafter or, if an appeal has been entered, while such appeal is pending.

An applicant may, under section 8(2), make applications at any time to the local authority for an alteration of the original conditions attached to the site licence as well as for an alteration of conditions imposed subsequently under section 8(1).

In *Peters v. Yiewsley and West Drayton U.D.C.*,[38] it was contended that, once twenty-eight days had elapsed since the original conditions were imposed, they could no longer be appealed against. The Divisional Court rejected that argument and held that a licence holder may wait and apply for an alteration of the original conditions at any time.

It is clear that the effect of the decision is that the time limit

---

[37] *Stewart v. Chapman* [1951] 2 K.B. 792 and see above, p. 49.
[38] [1963] 2 Q.B. 133; [1963] 1 All E.R. 843.

for appeals under section 7(1) can, in practice, be disregarded. An applicant may always present an appeal against site licence conditions by first applying to the local authority for an alteration and then, on refusal of his application, by appealing to the magistrates' court under section 8(2). Lord Parker C.J. foresaw this result but thought it not unreasonable "bearing in mind that these licences may last for a very long time".

Although the Act does not expressly state that an applicant must establish, on appeal, that an altered condition is unduly burdensome, it seems certain that the same test is applicable in the case of appeals against original and altered conditions. In the case of *Llanfyllin R.D.C. v. Holland*,[39] it was accepted that this was the test to be adopted. Moreover, the court is directed, as under section 7, on an appeal against altered conditions to have regard to any model standards.[40] No other specified criteria are laid down.

Fire Precautions

The local authority must consult the fire authority as to the extent to which any model standards relating to fire precautions are appropriate in relation to the site. Where no such standards have been specified or where the fire authority consider that the specified standards are inappropriate, the local authority must consult the fire authority as to what conditions relating to fire precautions should be attached to the site licence. In addition, the local authority must also consult the fire authority before altering any condition in a site licence that relates to fire precautions or before themselves providing a caravan site.[41]

---

[39] (1964) 190 E.G. 499; 62 L.G.R. 459.
[40] 1960 Act, s. 8(4). *Cf.* also the wording of s. 20(4) which, although concerned with existing sites, clearly relates s. 7 to s. 8.
[41] 1960 Act, ss. 5(3A) and (3B), 8(5) and 24(2A).

Exemptions from Site Licence Requirement

There are many instances in which a site licence is not required. These exceptions are important and should be noted carefully.

By virtue of section 2 of the 1960 Act, a site licence is not required for the use of land as a caravan site in any of the circumstances specified in the First Schedule to the Act.[42] These may be summarised as follows:

(1) Use Within Curtilage of a Dwelling House

No site licence is required if the use of land is incidental to the enjoyment as such of a dwelling house within the curtilage of which the land is situated.

In practice this is a popular exemption and one that will be of interest to the person owning a single caravan. The provision is clearly intended to cover the case of someone who places a caravan in his garden for the use of himself and his family. It would, therefore, extend to activities such as using the caravan to accommodate guests or children. It would not, presumably, include letting to strangers on a commercial basis.

(2) Use by a Person Travelling with a Caravan for One or Two Nights

This exemption extends to any person travelling with a caravan who brings it onto the land and stations it there for a period of not more than two nights.

In order for the exemption to apply, it is necessary that:

(i) there must be no other caravan on the land (or adjoining land), at the time; and

(ii) the land has not been used in this way for more than twenty-eight days in the preceding year.

---

[42] All the exceptions (except for use within the curtilage of a dwelling house) are subject to possible withdrawal.

*(3)   Use of Holdings of Five Acres or More in Certain
        Circumstances*

In certain circumstances, a site licence will not be necessary
for land which comprises, together with any adjoining
land which is in the same occupation and has not been
built on, not less than five acres.

The circumstances are that:

(i)   a caravan is not stationed thereon for more than
      twenty-eight days in the year; and

(ii) during that period not more than three caravans are
      stationed thereon.

The above requirements are subject to modification by
the Secretary of State. In particular, a smaller acreage may
be specified. To date, the Secretary of State has not
prescribed any modifications.

(4)   Sites Occupied and Supervised by Exempted Organisations

It is provided by paragraph 12 of Schedule 1 to the 1960
Act that the Secretary of State may grant a certificate of
exemption to any organisation where he is satisfied that its
objects include the encouragement or promotion of
recreational activities.

Where such an organisation has been granted a certificate
and occupies land as a caravan site, a licence is unnecessary
provided that the land is being used for the purpose of
recreation and that it is under the supervision of the
organisation.

Certificates of exemption have been issued to some 411
organisations, including national, regional and local bodies.
A list is available from the Countryside (Recreation &
Landscape) Division, DEFRA, Zone 1/03, Temple Quay
House, 2 The Square, Temple Quay, Bristol BS1 6EB.

(5)   Sites Approved by Exempted Organisations

Even where an exempted organisation does not occupy

the land, a site licence will not be required if the organisation in question has approved the land as a suitable site for use by its members for the purpose of recreation and certain conditions are fulfilled.

The conditions are:

(i) the organisation's approval must be contained in a certificate which must be given to the occupier of the land;

(ii) particulars of all certificates issued by the organisation must be sent to the Secretary of State;

(iii) certificates must specify the date of commencement and expiry. They may not be in force for more than one year;

(iv) no more than five caravans may be stationed on the land at any one time.

(6) Meetings Organised by Exempted Organisations
A site licence is not required for land which is being used for the purposes of a meeting of members of an exempted organisation so long as the meeting does not last for more than five days.

(7) Agricultural and Forestry Workers
A site licence is not required for land which is being used for the accommodation, during a particular season, of persons employed on the land in the same occupation (i.e. the site is occupied by the same person who occupies the land on which the seasonal workers are employed). In order to qualify for the exemption, it is necessary that the persons so employed are either: (i) employed in farming operations on agricultural land, or (ii) employed on land being used for the purpose of forestry.

It is to be observed that this exemption applies to temporary sites only. A permanent site for a caravan is not exempt, even where it is used only for providing accommodation for seasonal agricultural workers.[43]

(8) Building and Engineering Sites
Where land forms part of, or adjoins, land on which building or engineering operations are being carried out, a site licence is unnecessary for providing accommodation for persons employed in connection with those operations.

(9) Travelling Showmen
A site licence is not required for the use of land as a caravan site by a travelling showman provided that:

(i) he is a member of an organisation to which the Secretary of State has granted a certificate of recognition;

(ii) he is, at the time, travelling for the purpose of his business or has taken up winter quarters on the land between the beginning of October and the end of the following March.

The Secretary of State is empowered to grant a certificate to any organisation recognised by him as confining its membership to *bona fide* travelling showmen.[44] A certificate so granted may be withdrawn at any time.

(10) Sites Occupied by Licensing Authority[45]
No site licence is required where the land is occupied by the local authority in whose area the land is situated.

(11) Gypsy Sites Occupied by County Councils
No site licence is required where the land is occupied by a county council as a caravan site providing accommodation for gypsies.

---

[43] *North v. Brown* (1974) 231 E.G. 737.
[44] See DoE Circular 22/91 (WO Circular 78/91).
[45] This exemption is excluded for the purpose of defining a "protected site" under s. 1(2) of the Caravan Sites Act 1968; see ch. 9.

Power to Withdraw Certain Exemptions

The Secretary of State has the power to withdraw any certificates of exemption granted to various organisations as already outlined.[46]

In addition, upon the application of a local authority, the Secretary of State may make an order nullifying all or any of the exemptions in the Schedule in respect of the land specified in the order. Such order may subsequently be varied or revoked on the application of the local authority. Except in cases where an order is being revoked, the local authority must advertise the effect and the date of commencement of any order made by the Secretary of State in the *London* or *Edinburgh Gazette* (whichever is appropriate) and in a local newspaper.[47]

---

[46] 1960 Act, Sch. 1, paras. 10(2) and 12(2).
[47] 1960 Act, Sch. 1, para. 13.

Chapter 6

THE POWERS OF ENFORCEMENT OF LOCAL AUTHORITIES

General

The close connection between planning and site licence control effectively provides a stronger method of enforcement than a single scheme of control could hope to do. Where a person uses land as a caravan site without planning permission, he is subject to the same enforcement procedure as in the case of any other breach of planning permission (for which see below). In addition, however, as has been seen, he will be unable to obtain a site licence and will be subject to criminal proceedings under section 1(2) of the Caravan Sites and Control of Development Act 1960.[1]

In many cases, however, the breach will relate to one or more conditions of the relevant planning permission or site licence. Where this happens, the respective enforcement procedures may need to be invoked independently. It should be remembered that immunity from planning enforcement is not the same as immunity from planning permission. A formal grant of planning permission must always be obtained before a site licence can be granted.[1]

1.—ENFORCEMENT OF PLANNING PERMISSION

Planning Contravention Notice

Where it appears to a planning authority that there may have been a breach of planning control, the authority may serve a planning contravention notice on:

---

[1]   See ch. 3.

58

(1) The owner.

(2) The occupier.

(3) Any other person having an interest in the land.

(4) Anyone carrying out operations on the land or using it for any purpose.

The notice may require the person(s) served to give information about:

(i) any operations being carried out on the land, any use of the land or any other activities being carried out on the land; and

(ii) any matter relating to the conditions or limitations imposed by a grant of planning permission.

The respondent to a planning contravention notice has 21 days from the service of the notice to comply. The maximum penalty on conviction for breach of the notice is a fine not exceeding Level 3 on the standard scale (currently £1,000).

Power to Serve an Enforcement Notice

A local planning authority[2] may serve an enforcement notice where it appears to them that there has been a breach of planning control as defined by the 1990 Act. By section 171(A)(1) there is a breach of planning control if either: (i) development has been carried out without the grant of planning permission, or (ii) any conditions or limitations, subject to which the permission was granted, have not been complied with.

There is no obligation on the authority to serve an enforcement notice. Section 172 gives them a discretion to do so where they consider it expedient having regard to the provisions of the development plan and to any other material considerations.

---

[2] Defined in the Town and Country Planning Act 1990, s. 1.

It is very difficult to question the authority's discretion in the matter. It is clear that they do not have to satisfy themselves of a breach of planning control before serving the notice. The test of what is expedient is subjective and it seems that a *prima facie* case will suffice.[3]

The persons on whom the notice must be served are, by virtue of section 172(2):

(1) The owner.

(2) The occupier.

(3) Any other person having an interest in the land being an interest which, in the authority's opinion, is materially affected by the notice.

There has been some litigation on the question of whether a caravan dweller need be served with an enforcement notice.

In *Munnich v. Godstone R.D.C.*,[4] it was suggested that such a person could not be an occupier, within the meaning of the Act, if he were a licensee and therefore need not be served.

That dictum was not approved in *Stevens v. Bromley London Borough Council*.[5] In that case, a site operator had developed land as a caravan site without planning permission. Enforcement notices were served on him to restore the land to its former condition. They were also served on the respective caravan dwellers but not at the same time. It was held, by the Court of Appeal, that the caravan dwellers, even though they were licensees, were occupiers and should have been served at the same time as the site operator. The enforcement notices were invalid.

---

[3] *Miller-Mead v. Minister of Housing and Local Government* [1963] 2 Q.B. 196; [1963] 2 W.L.R. 225.
[4] [1966] 1 All E.R. 930; 64 L.G.R. 141.
[5] [1972] 1 All E.R. 712; (1971) 23 P. & C.R. 142.

It will always be prudent to serve enforcement notices on caravan dwellers. On any view, they are persons whose interest in the land is likely to be affected by the notices. In cases where the Mobile Homes Act 1983 applies,[6] there can be little doubt that they are occupiers within the meaning of the planning legislation.

The time within which a notice must be issued may be important. By virtue of section 171(B), it must be issued only within four years from the date of the breach of planning control where it relates to a breach consisting of:

(i) the carrying out without planning permission of building, engineering, mining or other operations in, on, over or under land; or

(ii) the making without planning permission of a change of use of any building to use as a single dwelling house.

In the case of any other breach of planning control, no enforcement action may be taken after ten years from the date of the breach.

By section 172(2) and (3) of the 1990 Act, a copy of the enforcement notice is required to be served not later than twenty-eight days before the date specified in the notice as the date on which it is to take effect, and not later than twenty-eight days after the date of its issue.

Where land is used as a caravan site for only part of the year, the four-year limitation will usually apply even though there is an apparent "change of use" every few months. The reason for this was explained in *Webber v. Minister of Housing and Local Government*.[7] In that case land had been used for more than four years as a caravan site in summer and for grazing in winter. It was held, by the Court of Appeal, that the land must be regarded as having a single

---

[6] See ch. 11.
[7] [1967] 3 All E.R. 981; 19 P. & C.R. 1. Whether the limitation applies is a different question.

use for two purposes, namely summer camping and winter grazing. Accordingly, an enforcement notice served within six months of the seasonal change was out of time because the land had been used in the same way for over four years.

An enforcement notice must specify:

(i)   the matters which appear to the local planning authority to constitute the breach of planning control; and

(ii) the paragraphs of section 171A(1) within which the breach falls, i.e. (a) carrying out development without the required planning permission, or (b) failing to comply with a condition or limitation subject to which the planning permission was granted.

The notice must also specify the steps which the authority require to be taken, in effect, to remedy the breach and the period within which the steps must be taken. The notice takes effect on the date specified in it. Service of the notice must take place within twenty-eight days after issue of the notice and not less than twenty-eight days before the date on which it is to take effect.[8]

If the notice does not comply with the statutory requirements, it is a nullity.[9] However, a notice may be valid if there are minor discrepancies which can be remedied on appeal.[10]

An enforcement notice can be withdrawn at any time and can be varied to waive or relax any requirement in the notice.[11]

In circumstances where an enforcement notice has taken effect and is, thereafter, not complied with there is, under section 179, as amended, a penalty for non-compliance,

[8]   1990 Act, s. 173.
[9]   *Miller-Mead v. Minister of Housing and Local Government* [1963] 2 Q.B. 196; [1963] 2 W.L.R. 225.
[10] *Coventry Scaffolding Co. (London) Ltd. v. Parker* [1987] J.P.L. 127.
[11] 1990 Act, s. 173A.

namely, on summary conviction a fine not exceeding £20,000 or on indictment a fine.

The Stop Notice

Section 183 provides that, where a planning authority have served an enforcement notice, they may, before that notice takes effect, serve a stop notice. This stop notice should refer to the enforcement notice and have a copy of it annexed to it. It may prohibit any person on whom it is served from carrying out or continuing any specified activity on the land, being any activity alleged in the enforcement notice to constitute a breach of planning control.

The operations which may be the subject of a stop notice are expressed to include the deposit of refuse or waste materials on land where that is a breach of planning control alleged in the enforcement notice. This has an obvious application in the case of caravan sites. A stop notice may not, however, prohibit the use of land as the site of a caravan occupied by any person as his only or main residence.

The notice may be served on any person whom the planning authority consider to have an interest in the land or to be concerned with the carrying out or continuance of any operations on the land. It can be seen that a stop notice may be served on a slightly wider class of persons than those contemplated under an enforcement notice.

There are fewer formalities required in relation to a stop notice. There is no prescribed form of notice.[12] Nor does it matter that a copy of the enforcement notice was not served on all the persons required to be served, provided that it is shown that the planning authority took all reasonably practicable steps to effect proper service.[13]

---

[12] A suitable form may be obtained from Shaw & Sons, Cat. No. TCP 137.
[13] 1990 Act, s. 184(8). In general it is not easy to challenge a stop notice because of alleged deficiencies in service. Its validity may, however, be challenged by applying for judicial review or in criminal proceedings arising out of failure to comply (see *R. v. Jenner* [1983] 2 All E.R. 46).

Section 184 states that a stop notice cannot take effect until the date specified in the notice. This may not be earlier than three, nor later than twenty-eight, days from the day on which the notice is first served on any person. In relation to any person served, it has effect from that date or the third day after service, whichever is the later. It lapses when the enforcement notice takes effect or is withdrawn or quashed.

The planning authority may withdraw a stop notice at any time by serving notice on those persons who were served with it. Where this happens, the stop notice ceases to have effect as from the date of service of the notice of withdrawal. The difference between this and an enforcement notice is that the enforcement notice can, as has been seen, only be withdrawn before it takes effect.

The penalties for non-compliance with a stop notice that has taken effect are, under section 187, the same as those in relation to an enforcement notice. Where, in such circumstances, a person carries out or causes or permits to be carried out operations prohibited by the notice, he is liable, on summary conviction, to a fine not exceeding £20,000; on indictment the extent of the fine is unlimited.

There is provision under the Act for compensation for loss attributable to a stop notice.[14] Disputes in relation to compensation are determined by the Lands Tribunal. It is to be noted that there is no appeal against a stop notice.

Enforcement of Conditions

Where planning permission has been granted subject to conditions and any of the conditions have not been complied with, the planning authority may serve a breach of condition notice on the person who is carrying out, or has carried out, the development or on any person having control of the land. The notice must require compliance

---

[14]   1990 Act, s. 186.

with the conditions specified in the notice and must set out the steps required to comply with the notice. The period for compliance must be specified and must be at least twenty-eight days from the service of the notice. Breach of a notice is an offence, for which the maximum penalty on conviction is a fine not exceeding Level 3 on the standard scale (currently £1,000).[15]

Injunctions

Where the planning authority consider it necessary or expedient for any actual or apprehended breach of planning control to be restrained by injunction, they may apply to the court (the High Court or the county court) for an injunction, whether or not they have used their other statutory powers.[16]

The Appeal Procedure

There is a right of appeal against an enforcement notice.[17] The time limit for appeal and the grounds thereof are set out in section 174. The section provides that the following persons may, within the time limit specified in the enforcement notice, appeal to the Secretary of State:

(1) The person(s) served with a copy of the enforcement notice.

(2) Any person having an interest in the land to which the notice relates.

(3) Any "relevant occupier", i.e. any person who occupies the land to which the notice relates by virtue of a licence and who continues so to occupy the land when the appeal is brought.

The main specified grounds of appeal are:

(i) planning permission ought to be granted for the

---

[15] 1990 Act, s. 187A.
[16] 1990 Act, s. 187B.
[17] 1990 Act, s. 174.

development, or a condition or limitation alleged to have been broken ought to be discharged;

(ii) the alleged breach of planning control has not taken place;

(iii) the matters alleged are not in breach of planning control;

(iv) the enforcement notice is out of time;

(v) copies of the enforcement notice were not served as required by section 172;

(vi) the steps required to be taken exceed what is necessary to remedy the breach or to remedy any injury to amenity caused by the breach;

(vii) the period for compliance with the notice falls short of what should reasonably be allowed.

There is no prescribed form of appeal. Notice of appeal must be in writing to the Secretary of State and must specify the grounds of appeal and give the information prescribed by regulations.[18]

Under section 289, the appellant or the planning authority may appeal to the High Court on a point of law only or require the Secretary of State to state and sign a case for the opinion of the High Court. The leave of the High Court is required before an appeal can proceed.

Certificate of Lawful Use or Development

Apart from the appeal procedure set out above, it is sometimes possible to resist an enforcement notice by obtaining a certificate of lawful use or development under section 191. For the purposes of the 1990 Act, a use or development is lawful if enforcement action cannot be

---

[18]   T.C.P. (Enforcement Notices and Appeals) Regulations 1991, S.I. 1991 No. 2804 (as amended).

taken against it, either because the time limit has run out or because no planning permission was required or for any other reason.

The time limits for taking enforcement action are prescribed by section 171B and are as follows:

(i) building and other operations: four years from the date on which the building or other works are substantially completed;

(ii) change of use of any building to a single dwelling house: four years from the date of the breach;

(iii) any other breach of planning control (including a change of use other than in (ii) above): ten years from the date of the breach.

A certificate granted under section 191 has effect as a grant of planning permission for the purposes of section 3(3) of the 1960 Act (see page 16 above).[19]

II.—ENFORCEMENT OF THE SITE LICENCE

It is now necessary to examine the various ways in which a local authority may ensure that conditions imposed under a site licence are complied with. All their remedies lie under the Caravan Sites and Control of Development Act 1960.

Power of Entry

One of the most important aspects of enforcement in relation to site licences, from the point of view of the local authority, is to know the extent of any breach of condition and decide what action it may be necessary to take.

Accordingly, section 26(1) of the 1960 Act provides that authorised officers of the authority have the right to enter,

---

[19] 1990 Act, s. 191(7).

at all reasonable hours, land which is used as a caravan site or in respect of which an application for a site licence has been made.

Before the right can be exercised, however, twenty-four hours' notice of the intended entry must be given to the occupier. If required to do so, an officer must produce a duly authenticated document showing his authority. It is, therefore, essential that officers are equipped with the necessary documentation.

The only circumstances under which an authority may exercise their power of entry are, by section 26(1), expressed to be for the purpose of:

(1) Determining what conditions should be attached to a site licence, or whether conditions attached to a site licence should be altered.

(2) Ascertaining whether there is, or has been, on or in connection with the land any contravention of the provisions of the 1960 Act dealing with caravan sites.

(3) Ascertaining whether or not circumstances exist which would authorise the local authority to take any action, or execute any work authorised by the Act.

(4) Taking any action, or executing any work authorised by the Act.

In certain circumstances, a local authority may apply to a justice of the peace for a warrant authorising them, by any authorised officer, to enter the land, if need be by force. Before such a warrant may be issued, two matters must be established to the satisfaction of a justice of the peace, namely that:

(i) admission to the land has been refused, or that a refusal is expected, or that the occupier is temporarily absent, or that an application for admission would defeat the object of the entry; *and*

(ii) there is reasonable ground for entering on the land for any of the reasons authorised by section 26(1).[20]

It is, by section 26(5) of the Act, an offence wilfully to obstruct any person acting in the execution of the general power. There is liability on summary conviction to a fine not exceeding Level 1 on the standard scale (currently £200).

Power to Execute Works

This remedy applies only to conditions imposed under a site licence that require certain work to be carried out. In cases where such a condition has been imposed and not complied with, the local authority are empowered, under section 9(3) of the 1960 Act, to carry out the work themselves. They are entitled to recover any expenses reasonably incurred from the occupier of the land as a simple contract debt.

It will be recalled that similar powers are available to an occupier of land subject to a licence or to a tenancy of not more than four hundred square yards in area.[21] Such a person, under section 12(2), has the right – as against a person claiming under the licence or tenancy – to enter on the land and do anything reasonably required for the purpose of complying with any conditions attaching to the site licence.

The above power is wider than that available to a local authority because it applies to all kinds of condition under a site licence, and not merely to those requiring work to be carried out. On the other hand, local authorities have more varied means of enforcement at their disposal (see below), and bear the ultimate responsibility of enforcing conditions against the occupier himself.

---

[20]   1960 Act, s. 26(2).
[21]   i.e. in accordance with the definition of "occupier" under s. 1(3) of the 1960 Act; and see ch. 3.

Penalty for Breaking Conditions

In relation to most breaches of condition under a site licence, the local authority's means of enforcement are cumulative. In the first instance they may take proceedings in the local magistrates' court. At a later stage they may, in certain circumstances, apply to the same court for the site licence to be revoked (see below).

Section 9(1) of the Act makes it an offence for a site licence holder to fail to comply with any conditions attached to the licence. There is liability, on summary conviction, to a fine not exceeding Level 4 on the standard scale (currently £2,500).

In *Penton Park Homes Ltd. v. Chertsey U.D.C.*,[22] it was held that the offence created by the Act is a continuing one. In that case the appellant was held to be rightly convicted of failing to comply with a site licence condition requiring him to carry out work within twelve months from the grant of the licence. This was so even though the charge was not laid until over four years from the expiration of the twelve-month period.

Revocation of Site Licence

If a site licence holder continues to break conditions, the local authority may, instead of prosecuting him for those breaches, apply to the magistrates' court to have his licence revoked. Where revocation is ordered, another licence may not be issued in respect of land to the same holder for at least three years.[23]

Revocation is a drastic remedy. Before such an order can be made certain conditions must be satisfied. They are:

(1) Revocation may only be ordered by the court before whom a person is convicted for breach of a condition.

---

[22] (1973) 26 P. & C.R. 531.
[23] 1960 Act, s. 3(6); see ch. 5.

(2) At the time that the order is made there must have been two or more previous occasions on which a person has been so convicted. There must, therefore, be a total of at least three convictions before an order can be made.[24]

An order of revocation comes into effect on the date that the court specifies in it. This must not be earlier than the expiration of any period within which notice of appeal may be given against the conviction. Where an appeal is entered within the required time,[25] the order has no effect until the appeal is finally determined or else withdrawn.[26]

It is possible for either the local authority or the person whose licence has been ordered to be revoked to apply to the magistrates' court to extend the date on which the order is to come into force. It appears that an extension of time may only be granted if adequate notice of the application has been given to the other side.[27] Where such notice is given, the court has a discretion.

---

[24] 1960 Act, s. 9(2).
[25] i.e. 21 days after the day on which the court's decision was given: 1960 Act, s. 9(2).
[26] 1960 Act, s. 9(2).
[27] 1960 Act, s. 9(2).

Chapter 7

THE DUTIES AND RESPONSIBILITIES OF LOCAL AUTHORITIES

In this chapter it is proposed to examine some powers and duties of local authorities in relation to caravan sites. Although one of their most important duties arises towards gypsies, this has become such a controversial topic, and one more connected with security of tenure than with site licence control, that it is thought more appropriate to include it separately.[1]

Provision of Caravan Sites

By virtue of section 24(1) of the Caravan Sites and Control of Development Act 1960, local authorities (i.e. county councils, district councils, London borough councils, the Common Council of the City of London and the Council of the Isles of Scilly in England and county and county borough councils in Wales) have power, in their area, to provide sites where caravans may be brought for holiday or other temporary purposes, or for use as permanent residences. They are also entitled to manage the sites or to lease them to others. Section 24(7), however, states that they have no power to provide caravans.

In exercising their powers under section 24, the local authority may, under section 24(2), do anything appearing to them desirable, and they may in particular:

(i) acquire land which is in use as a caravan site or which has been laid out as a caravan site;

(ii) provide for the use of those occupying caravan sites any services or facilities for their health or convenience.

---

[1] See Part III.

The local authority are directed, in respect of whatever measures they take, to have regard to the model standards.[2] They may impose such reasonable charges, for what they provide, as they think fit.[3]

In relation to their provision of services or facilities, section 24(4) states that these may be made available to those who do not normally reside in the area as much as to those who do.

So far as the acquiring of land is concerned, this may be done either by agreement or compulsorily. By section 24(5) of the Act, a local authority may acquire land by means of compulsory purchase where it appears to them either:

(i)   that a caravan site, or an additional site, is needed in the area; or

(ii) that it is in the interests of users of caravans that land in use as a site should be taken over.

The prior authorisation of the Secretary of State is needed for this. If forthcoming, the procedure to be followed is as set out in the Acquisition of Land Act 1981.[4]

The power of compulsory purchase, for example, in this context has been described as "a long stop provision" which would only be exercised where either:

(i)   there was a real shortage of privately operated sites; or

(ii) a site was so bad or neglected that, in the interests of the caravan dwellers, the local authority were obliged to take over and manage the site themselves.

It is apparent, nonetheless, that local authorities are under a responsibility to provide caravan sites under the 1960

---

[2]   1960 Act, s. 24(2); see Appendices A and B, pp. 163 and 173.
[3]   1960 Act, s. 24(3).
[4]   1960 Act, s. 24(6).

Act. That responsibility is no less important, in circumstances where it is required to be exercised, merely because the provisions creating it give rise to a power rather than a duty.

Prohibition of Caravans on Commons

Even before the passing of the 1960 Act, it was not easy to take a caravan on to a common and inhabit it. In particular, there were two well-established statutory restrictions. These still apply and are:

(1) *The Law of Property Act 1925, section 193(4)*. This gives members of the public the right of access for air and exercise over certain commons and waste lands. There is a prohibition, however, against any person who, without lawful authority, draws or drives upon land to which the section applies any carriage, cart, caravan, truck or other vehicle, or who camps or lights any fire on such land. In general, the section applies to commons in urban areas.

(2) *The Commons Act 1899, Part I*. The purpose of Part I of this Act is to enable schemes to be made for the regulation and management of certain commons. Byelaws have frequently been made under such schemes. Many of these byelaws contain a prohibition against bringing caravans, without lawful authority, on to commons to which the scheme applies.[5]

Sections 23(1) and (2) of the Act provide that, apart from the exceptions referred to in (1) and (2) immediately above and also where a current site licence is in force, district councils may make orders prohibiting, either wholly or in part, the stationing of caravans for the purpose of human habitation on any land in their area which is or forms part of a common. Such orders may be

---

[5]   Section 34 of the Road Traffic Act 1988 contains prohibitions that have a practical application to caravans; see ch. 16.

revoked or varied at any time by a subsequent order to that effect.[6] For the purpose of the Act, the word "common" is, by section 23(8), expressed to include any land subject to be enclosed under the Inclosure Acts 1845 to 1882, and any town or village green.

Where such an order has been made, it is an offence for any person to station a caravan on land to which the order applies. There is liability, on summary conviction, to a fine not exceeding Level 1 on the standard scale (currently £200).

District councils have a duty to take all reasonable steps to ensure that copies of orders made under section 23 are so displayed on the land affected as to give adequate warning of the existence of the order to persons entering on the land. They have the right to place on the land any notices that they consider necessary.[7]

The Second Schedule to the Act contains further provisions concerning orders relating to commons. Particular matters dealt with include the requirement that orders must be advertised beforehand by means of notices published in one or more local newspapers, and the allowing of objections to be made within twenty-eight days of such notice first being published.

Public Health Control

The 1960 Act enables local authorities to impose wide-ranging conditions relating to public health matters, under a site licence.

The nature and extent of the conditions that may be attached to a site licence have been discussed in an earlier chapter.[8] In the context of public health, Danckwerts L.J. (in the Court of Appeal) emphasised in *Chertsey U.D.C. v.*

---

6   1960 Act, s. 23(5).
7   1960 Act, s. 23(4).
8   Ch. 5.

Mixnam's Properties[9] that conditions should secure "the provision of proper facilities in respect of sanitation and amenities so that the site should not become a menace to the health of the occupants of the caravans or other persons".

In addition, it will be recalled that section 5(1) of the 1960 Act, in laying down specific conditions that may be imposed under a site licence, specifies conditions "for securing and maintaining adequate sanitary and other facilities, services and equipment".[10]

Notwithstanding the powers contained in the 1960 Act, there remain parts of the Public Health Act 1936 that may still be applied to caravans. Certain of these provisions may need to be invoked where, for example, conditions under a site licence are either silent about public health matters or are not wide enough to cover the contingency in question. There are also certain caravans and sites that are exempt from the requirement of a site licence[11] and, in such cases, the older form of public health control will be important. District councils (including London borough councils, the Common Council of the City of London, the Sub Treasurer of the Inner Temple and the Under Treasurer of the Middle Temple) in England and county and county borough councils in Wales are the local authorities with the prime responsibility for carrying out the purposes of the 1936 Act.

The authorities' power under the 1936 Act derive, in the first instance, from section 268 thereof. Section 268(1) expressly applies certain other parts of the Act to caravans used for human habitation.

The parts of the Act so applied which may be relevant to caravans and caravan sites are:

---

[9]   [1963] 3 W.L.R. 38 (i.e. the Court of Appeal judgment).
[10]   *Cf.* also Model Standards, DoE Circular 14/89 (WO Circular 23/89).
[11]   See ch. 5.

Part of the Act	**Subject Matter**
Part II (ss. 83-86)	Filthy or verminous premises or articles and verminous persons.
Part V	Prevention, notification and treatment of disease.
Part XII	General.

Provision formerly in Part III of the 1936 Act are now to be found in Part III of the Environmental Protection Act 1990 (EPA 1990) which covers statutory nuisances and clean air.

Apart from the above provisions, by virtue of section 268(4) district councils have the power to make byelaws for promoting cleanliness in, and the habitable condition of, caravans used for human habitation, for preventing the spread of infectious disease by the occupants or other users, and generally for the prevention of nuisances.

The most important aspect of public health control, so far as caravans are concerned, is contained in Part III of the Environmental Protection Act 1990 dealing with nuisances.

A statutory nuisance is defined by section 268(2) of the 1936 Act to mean (in the context of caravan law) a caravan:

(a) which is in such a state, or so overcrowded as to be prejudicial to the health of the inmates;[12] or

(b) the use of which, by reason of the absence of proper sanitary accommodation[13] or otherwise, gives rise, whether on the site or on other land, to a nuisance or to conditions prejudicial to health.

There is a duty on every local authority to cause their district to be inspected from time to time for the detection

---

[12] "Prejudicial to health" means "injurious or likely to cause injury, to health", EPA 1990, s. 79(7).
[13] This expression is not defined in the Act.

78 The Duties and Responsibilities of Local Authorities

of statutory nuisances.[14] Where an authority are satisfied of the existence of such a nuisance, there are various remedies available to them. The provisions relating to these remedies are complicated and an outline only is given here.

(1) Abatement Notices
Subject to certain exceptions (for which see below), an authority satisfied of the existence of a statutory nuisance are directed to serve an abatement notice. This is a notice requiring the person on whom it is served to abate the nuisance or to execute such works and take such steps as may be necessary for that purpose.[15]

The classes of person on whom abatement notices should be served are as follows:

(a) A nuisance under section 268(2)(a):

    (i) the person who caused the nuisance must be served;

    (ii) if that person cannot be found, the owner or occupier of the premises on which the nuisance arose must be served. For this purpose, the expression "occupier" includes the person in charge of the caravan;

    (iii) where the nuisance arises from any defect of a structural character, the owner of the premises must, in any event, be served.[16]

(b) A nuisance under section 268(2)(b):

    (i) as in (i)-(iii) above;

    (ii) there is also a discretion to serve the occupier of the land on which the caravan is erected or

---

[14] EPA 1990. s. 79(1).
[15] EPA 1990, s. 80.
[16] EPA 1990, s. 80.

stationed. Where an occupier of the land is so served, it is a defence for him to prove that he did not authorize the caravan to be stationed or erected on his land.[17]

Where an abatement notice has not been complied with, the local authority may abate the nuisance and do whatever is necessary in execution of the notice.[18] The authority are entitled to recover the costs they reasonably incur in abating or preventing the recurrence of the nuisance.[19]

(2) Summary Proceedings
Where a person on whom an abatement notice is served, without reasonable excuse, contravenes or fails to comply with any requirement or prohibition imposed by the notice, he is liable on summary conviction to a fine not exceeding Level 5 on the standard scale (currently £5,000) and a further fine of one tenth of that level for each day on which the offence continues after conviction.[20]

Where proceedings are taken in relation to section 268(3) of the 1936 Act (see above), the court may make an order prohibiting the use for human habitation of a caravan at such places or within such areas as may be specified in the order.[21]

(3) High Court Proceedings
In certain circumstances, an authority may elect to institute proceedings in the High Court rather than summarily.

Section 81(5) of the Environmental Protection Act 1990 provides that, where an authority are of the opinion that summary proceedings would afford an inadequate remedy, they may take proceedings in the High Court for the

---

[17] Public Health Act 1936, s. 268(3).
[18] 1990 Act, s. 81(3).
[19] 1990 Act, s. 81(4).
[20] 1990 Act, s. 80(5).
[21] 1936 Act, s. 268(5). This order may also be made in respect of a breach of a byelaw.

purpose of securing the abatement or prohibition of any statutory nuisance. Such proceedings may be instituted despite the fact that the authority may have suffered no damage from the nuisance.

(4) Defective Premises
Apart from the remedies referred to, there are some situations in which an authority is permitted to carry out work by themselves without serving an abatement notice.

By virtue of section 76(1) of the Building Act 1984, this may be done if it appears to the authority that:

(a) any premises are in such a state as to be prejudicial to health or a nuisance; and

(b) there would be unreasonable delay in remedying the defective state by following the summary procedure or abatement notice procedure.

Before an authority may carry out such works, they must serve, on the person who would normally have been served with an abatement notice, a notice stating that they intend to remedy the defective state.[22] There is a provision in the Act for a person so served to serve a counter notice of intention to remedy the defective state.[23] Unless this is done, the authority may carry out the necessary work themselves and recover any expenses reasonable incurred.[24]

(5) Building Regulations (in relation to Mobile Homes)
In most cases, building regulations currently in force under the Building Act 1984 will not apply to mobile homes. Where, however, a mobile home has been altered so that it is no longer capable of being moved, it is submitted that it might then be a "building" to which such regulations would apply.

---

[22] Building Act 1984, s. 76(1).
[23] Building Act 1984, s. 76(3).
[24] Building Act 1984, s. 76(2).

By virtue of section 121(2) of the Building Act 1984, a building for which regulations may be made includes a "structure or erection of whatever kind or nature", including a "moveable object of any kind". The ambit of such regulations would extend to most types of mobile homes, whether capable of being moved or not.

Part II

CARAVANS AS HOMES

Chapter 8

THE SCHEME OF LEGISLATION

This part of the book concerns the legislation affecting residential occupiers of caravans and mobile homes.

The principal Acts are the Caravan Sites Act 1968 (excluding gypsies) and the Mobile Homes Act 1983. Although both these Acts seek to protect residential occupiers, there are significant differences both as to the nature of the protection afforded and as to the persons entitled to that protection.

In this chapter it is proposed, first, to consider two distinctions that frequently mystify both occupiers and site operators alike. They are:

(1) The distinction between a caravan and a mobile home.

(2) The distinction between owning and renting a caravan or mobile home.

Thereafter an outline of the legislation is given before turning to the detailed provisions.

When Does a Caravan Become a Mobile Home?

As has been seen, the Caravan Sites and Control of Development Act 1960 is solely concerned with the licensing and control of caravan sites. The term "caravan site" connotes habitation rather than residence[1] and, therefore, the 1960 Act does not provide any measure of security of tenure for persons occupying caravans as their homes. In *Chertsey U.D.C. v. Mixnam's Properties,*[2] an attempt by the council to impose conditions relating to security of tenure was rejected by the House of Lords.

---

[1]   1960 Act, s. 1(4); see above, p. 20.
[2]   [1964] 2 All E.R. 627; 15 P. & C.R. 331; see ch. 5.

When most caravans were constructed and used for holiday purposes, the provision of adequate security was unimportant. For the most part, occupiers of such structures simply held a licence for the pitch of land on which their caravans stood from the site operator. That was enough.

With the advent of the modern mobile home, however, this became wholly inappropriate. In practice, a mobile home is usually far from mobile.[3] It frequently has no wheels and is more akin to a bungalow or chalet than to a caravan. Most important, mobile homes now serve as permanent homes for large numbers of people. They want something more than a mere licence.

In attempting to understand the legislation that follows, the practical distinction between the traditional touring caravan and the permanency of the mobile home should always be borne in mind. In a nutshell, the idea behind the 1968 and 1983 Acts can be summarised in the phrase "caravans as homes".

It should be clearly understood, however, that a "mobile home" has, in law, exactly the same meaning as a "caravan".[4] Not all mobile homes are modern, self-contained units. Older residences may well have served, in the past, as touring caravans. The term "mobile home" is helpful in understanding the scheme behind the current legislation but it may be seriously misleading if thought to consist of an entirely separate species in law.

Whether a caravan (including a mobile home) is protected under the 1968 and 1983 Acts depends upon concepts of residence and (in the latter case) ownership. It is immaterial whether the structure occupied is a "mobile home" in the popular understanding of that term. Thus it is, theoretically, possible for the owner of a camper van or disused railway

---

[3]   Note the comments of Lord Denning M.R. in *Taylor v. Calvert* [1978] 2 All E.R. 630.
[4]   1983 Act, s. 5(1); see p. 95.

coach to be protected under the Acts because both structures are capable of being "caravans" within the meaning of section 29 of the 1960 Act (as amended).[5]

Owning and Renting a Caravan: the Differences in Law

Most people who live in mobile homes own their homes but do not ordinarily own or lease the land on which they are stationed. A minority of occupiers, however, lease the mobile home as well as the pitch. The lessor of the structure may be either the site operator or some independent third party.

The 1983 Act is, essentially, restricted to the owner occupier who lives in the mobile home as his main residence. Nowhere in the Act is it provided that the occupier must actually own the structure but this is implicit from the fact that security of tenure is afforded only to those persons who are entitled both to station a mobile home on site and to occupy it as their only or main residence.[6]

In almost every case, this category will only apply to the owner of a mobile home because it is the owner rather than the person who merely rents who is entitled to station the structure on site.

If the owner of the mobile home is the site operator, it is apparent that he alone is entitled to station it on the site. The same is likely to be true if a third party is the owner. He will have an arrangement (probably a licence) with the site operator permitting him to station the mobile home on the operator's land. It will be a wholly exceptional case where the rental agreement itself permits the occupier of the mobile home, rather than the owner, to station it on site because such an agreement would need the concurrence of the site operator.

---

[5]   See p. 20.
[6]   1983 Act, s. 1(1).

Under current legislation, the owner of a mobile home who decides to let the structure may be in an invidious position. If he previously occupied it as a home himself, he loses the protection of the 1983 Act but does not pass any protection to the lessee for the reasons stated above. It seems probable, however, that the letting of the structure confers an assured tenancy or an assured shorthold tenancy under the Housing Acts 1988 and 1996.[7]

If, during the course of the tenancy, the site operator decides to terminate the owner's licence to station the structure on site,[8] the owner would be in breach of the terms of his licence by refusing to comply with a proper notice. On the other hand, by complying he would be in breach of his obligations, as landlord, to the occupier of the mobile home.[9]

The 1968 Act is wider in scope. It is intended to apply both to those who rent as well as to those who own their homes. The category of persons protected is, by section 1(1), expressed to cover a person entitled to station the structure on site and occupy it as his residence or to occupy as his residence a structure already stationed on site.

It is, perhaps, unfortunate that the two Acts are not aimed at protecting an identical class of persons and that, in particular, the 1983 Act does not extend to persons who lease their homes.[10] Not only would the anomalies referred to above have been removed but the Acts themselves would have been far less confusing.

The Caravan Sites Act 1968

The object of the 1968 Act is to confer on all permanent

---

[7] *R. v. Rent Officer of Nottinghamshire Registration Area ex parte Allen* [1985] 52 P. & C.R. 41.

[8] The site operator would have to serve written notice on the occupier of the mobile home under s. 2 of the 1968 Act; see p. 100.

[9] For breach, e.g. of the implied covenant of quiet enjoyment.

[10] Admittedly a number of provisions would need revising, e.g. provisions for sale and commission.

occupiers of caravans,[11] whether they lease or own their homes, protection against summary eviction and harassment. It achieves this, essentially, by making such acts criminal offences.

Wrongful eviction is the enforcement, otherwise than by proceedings in the county court, of any right to exclude the occupier from the site or the caravan or to remove the caravan from the site.[12] Where, in eviction proceedings, the court makes an order, it may suspend the operation of that order for up to twelve months[13] unless the proceedings were begun by a local authority or in a case where there is no site licence in force in respect of the site.[14] Where an order is so suspended, the court may impose whatever conditions it thinks reasonable, including stipulations as to payment of arrears of rent.[15]

The offence of harassment is committed by acting in a way calculated to affect the peace or comfort of the occupier or persons residing with him, or by the persistent withdrawal or withholding of services or facilities reasonably required.[16]

These basic protections are supplemented by the requirement that site owners must, except under fixed term agreements, given a minimum of four weeks' notice to the occupier to vacate the site.[17]

The cumulative effect of the above provisions is that the permanent resident of a caravan must be served with proper notice and, thereafter, has the right to remain on site until such time as he is dispossessed by the court. The specific provisions of the 1968 Act will be considered in

---

[11] Including, of course, mobile homes (see above).
[12] 1968 Act, ss. 3 and 5.
[13] 1968 Act, s. 4.
[14] 1968 Act, s. 4(6).
[15] 1968 Act, s. 4(2).
[16] 1968 Act, s. 3(1).
[17] 1968 Act, s. 2.

more detail later on in Chapter 10. Even at this stage, however, it can be seen that the protection afforded by the Act is very limited. It really amounts to an extension of time in which to leave and protection from interference within that time. There is, in particular, no security of tenure. If the occupier has to rely upon the 1968 Act alone, his position is not much better than that of a mere licensee. It was with that in mind that the mobile homes legislation was developed.

The Mobile Homes Act 1983

The 1983 Act affects permanent residential occupiers of caravans. It does not (unlike the 1968 Act) apply to persons merely renting the caravan but is restricted to owner occupiers[18] who rent the pitch on which the structure stands from the site operator. Similarly, the Act does not cover touring caravans or mobile homes used for holiday purposes.

Most caravan sites come under the ambit of the 1983 Act because it is expressed to apply to those sites which require a site licence under the 1960 Act.[19] Local authority sites are also included but gypsy sites are specifically excluded.[20]

As soon as an occupier becomes entitled to station and occupy, as his residence, a mobile home on site, he has an agreement to which the 1983 Act applies. There is automatic security of tenure as soon as the occupier agrees to come on site because the Act implies a number of important terms that ensure, *inter alia*, that he has indefinite security unless and until the site owner is successful in an application to the court to terminate the agreement.[21] Other terms automatically implied include the right to sell a mobile home on site or to give it to a member of the occupier's

---

[18] This is implicit in the way in which the Act is phrased. See 1983 Act, s. 1(1) and above at pp. 87-88.
[19] 1983 Act, s. 5(1).
[20] 1983 Act, s. 5(1).
[21] 1983 Act, s. 2(1) and Part I Sch. I.

family and provisions as to the resiting of the structure.[22]

Few of the terms implied by the Act are of direct benefit to the site owner. In this way, the onus is placed upon him to negotiate express terms in relation to pitch fees, obligations of the occupier as to repair and maintenance and related matters.

There is a requirement under the 1983 Act on the site owner to serve a written statement on the occupier setting out all the express and implied terms of the agreement between them.[23] If the site owner fails to serve the written statement, the various implied terms will bind him in any event.

The statement is required to be served within three months of the date that the occupier becomes entitled to come onto the site. In a case where the site owner and occupier had entered into an agreement prior to the 20th May 1983 (the date of the Act coming into force), the period for serving the statement was six months from 20th May.[24]

Where the site owner fails to serve the written statement, there is no sanction on him. The occupier may, however, apply to the court for an order that he serve it.[25] If there is a dispute as to any of the terms set out in the statement, either party may apply to the court, provided that they do so within six months of the giving of the statement, and the court may either imply certain further terms or else order that express terms contained in the statement be either varied or deleted.[26]

Finally, the following important points should be noted:

(1) The 1983 Act applies to all occupiers even where they

---

[22]   1983 Act, s. 2(1) and Part I Sch. I.
[23]   1983 Act, s. 1(2).
[24]   1983 Act, s. 1(2) and (3).
[25]   1983 Act, s. 1(5). This application may be made at any time.
[26]   1983 Act, s. 2(2) and (3).

may have had, or still have, the benefit of an agreement under the (largely repealed) Mobile Homes Act 1975 or any other agreement whether oral or written.[27]

(2) Terms implied by the Act override contrary written terms or verbal agreements.[28]

(3) The occupiers' security of tenure is limited only by:

(a) any limitation by virtue of planning permission or on the length of the period of the site owner's interest in the site;[29]

(b) the court being satisfied on one of a limited number of grounds necessary for the granting of an eviction order.[30] These relate to a breach of agreement on the part of the occupier, situations where the occupier no longer occupies the mobile home as his only or main residence and cases where the structure is, by reason of its age and condition, having or likely to have a detrimental effect on site amenities. Even then, the court may suspend the operation of any eviction order for up to twelve months.[31]

(4) The occupier need do nothing at all to be protected under the 1983 Act. Provided that he qualifies for security, he will have it merely by occupying the caravan on site.

(5) Care should be taken, however, once the written statement is received. This must be in a specified form[32] and will inform the occupier about his rights.

---

[27] Assuming, of course, that such occupiers qualify for protection under the Act; see 1983 Act, s. 1(1)-(3).
[28] 1983 Act, s. 2(1).
[29] 1983 Act, Part I of Sch. I para. 2.
[30] 1983 Act, Part I of Sch. I para. 4.
[31] Caravan Sites Act 1968, s. 4(1); see p. 106.
[32] 1983 Act, s. 1(2)(e) and (6). See the Mobile Homes (Written Statement) Regulations 1983, S.I. 1983 No. 1749.

As stated above, it will probably contain a number of express terms. The site owner and owner alike have only a limited time (six months) to challenge these terms. If they fail to act within that period, it seems that they will be debarred, thereafter, from seeking to oppose them.

Residential Tenancies Subject to Statutory Control

The law relating to the statutory control of residential tenancies is complex and outside the scope of this book. Until 1989, the main residential control was to be found in the Rent Act 1977. Residential tenancies granted before 15th January 1989 are generally subject to the 1977 Act and are referred to as regulated tenancies. Residential tenancies granted on or after that date are subject to the Housing Act 1988 and are referred to as assured tenancies, of which the commonest form is an assured shorthold tenancy. An assured tenancy granted after 27th February 1997 is an assured shorthold tenancy save in very restricted circumstances.[33]

Strangely, it has never been finally decided whether or not a caravan is a dwelling-house for the purpose of legislation controlling residential tenancies. The balance of opinion seems to be that it can be, provided that there is a sufficient degree of permanence.[34]

It is submitted that it will be a question of fact in each case depending, primarily, upon immobility or intended immobility of the structure. A modern mobile home is more likely to be subject to the statutory controls over residential tenancies than a touring caravan which is, in fact, lived in as a home by the occupier.

Assuming that a particular caravan or mobile home is so subject, the consequences for the occupier will, in all

---

[33]   Housing Act 1996, s. 96.
[34]   *R. v. Rent Officer of Nottinghamshire Registration Area ex parte Allen* [1985] 52 P. & C.R. 41; *Norton v. Knowles* [1969] 1 Q.B. 572.

probability, depend upon who has let out the structure to him.[35] If the lessor is the site owner, it is likely that the tenancy is an assured tenancy or an assured shorthold tenancy. Broadly speaking, residential tenancies granted after 14th January 1989 fall into these categories.[36]

Where, however, the caravan has been leased out by a third party, the position in law will be more complicated. Although the occupier is entitled to the same protection as against the lessor, his rights as against the site owner who wants possession are less obvious. It may well be the case that the site owner is entitled to an eviction order against the original lessor under the 1968 Act. Although, as against his lessor, the occupier may have the protection of an assured tenancy, that protection will avail him little if the lessor is obliged, under an eviction order, to remove his caravan from the site. In such circumstances, the occupier's remedy would appear to lie against the lessor in damages. There is, however, a conflict between caravan and residential tenancy legislation that awaits clarification by the courts.

---

[35]   If he owns the caravan he will not, of course, be protected. It is only if the dwelling is let out to him that there can be any possibility of the statutory controls applying.

[36]   See ch. 12.

Chapter 9

DEFINITIONS

The terms considered here are those that occur in the Caravan Sites Act 1968 and Mobile Homes Act 1983. Both Acts employ similar terminology. Although identical words are often used, they do not always mean the same thing. Reference should, therefore, be made to this chapter as a complement to later analysis.

Caravans and Mobile Homes

This is the one instance where the Acts use different expressions. The 1968 Act refers to "caravans" whereas the 1983 Act uses the term "mobile homes".

It cannot be emphasised enough, however, that although different words are used both Acts contemplate exactly the same type of structure.[1]

The expression "caravan" was comprehensively defined in the 1960 Act. That definition was amended by the 1968 Act so as to include twin-unit caravans.[2] The same definition is preserved in the 1983 Act.[3] Although the 1983 Act uses a different expression, it is expressly provided by section 5(1) thereof that "mobile home" has the same meaning as "caravan" in the earlier Acts.

To the layman it will seem strange that wholly dissimilar trading terms should be equated in law. The reason for this is probably that it is permanent residence, rather than whether a particular structure is better described as a caravan or mobile home, that lies at the heart of the legislation. It is submitted, however, that it would have been preferable for the Acts to have retained uniformity of expression.

---

[1] This point is developed in more detail above at pp. 85-86.
[2] 1960 Act, s. 29(1), as amended by s. 13(1) of the 1968 Act, and see ch. 3.
[3] *Cf.* 1968 Act, s. 16 and 1983 Act, s. 5(1).

Protected Site

A "protected site" is, for the purpose of both Acts, expressed to mean any land in respect of which a site licence is required under Part I of the 1960 Act.[4] A site is, however, not "protected" if the land in question has a relevant planning permission or site licence which is either:

(i) expressed to be granted for holiday use only; or

(ii) otherwise so expressed or subject to such conditions that there are times of the year when no caravan or mobile home may be stationed on the land for human habitation.[5]

Caravan sites operated by a local authority are in a slightly different position under the 1968 and 1983 Acts. Such sites do not require a site licence.[6] They are, however, included within the definition of the term "protected site" under both Acts.[7]

The only difference is that, under section 5(1) of the 1983 Act, land occupied by a local authority as a caravan site providing accommodation for gypsies[8] is not protected. This means that gypsies enjoying such accommodation are restricted to the somewhat limited benefits afforded by the 1968 Act and are not entitled to the much greater security of tenure provisions contained in the 1983 Act.

Residential Contract

This is a term peculiar to the Caravan Sites Act 1968. It is, however, necessary to an understanding of other definitions.

---

[4]   This will, apparently, mean that a site is "protected" even where no site licence will be granted; it is sufficient that one is required. See *Hooper v. Eaglestone* (1977) 245 *Estates Gazette* 572, D.C.
[5]   *Cf.* 1968 Act, s. 1(2) and 1983 Act, s. 5(1).
[6]   1960 Act, Sch. 1 para. 11.
[7]   *Cf.* 1968 Act, s. 1(2) and 1983 Act, s. 5(1).
[8]   There is an analagous exclusion for Scotland.

By virtue of section 1(1) of that Act, the security of tenure provisions apply in relation to any licence or contract, whenever entered into, under which a person is entitled:

(i) to station a caravan on a protected site and occupy it as his residence; or

(ii) to occupy as his residence a caravan stationed on a protected site.

Such a licence or contract is known as a "residential contract" and is clearly intended to apply equally to persons who rent pitches on caravan sites as well as to those who rent both caravans and pitches.

In this context, it should be observed that a person's residence is where, in ordinary language, he lives.[9] It is perfectly possible to be resident in more than one place at the same time.[10]

Owner and Occupier

The definition of "owner" is virtually the same under both the 1968 and 1983 Acts.

For the purpose of the 1968 Act, the owner of a protected site is, by section 1(3), expressed to mean the person who is or would, apart from any residential contract, be entitled to possession of the land.

Section 5(1) of the 1983 Act provides that the term "owner" means, in relation to a protected site, the person who, by virtue of an estate or interest held by him, is entitled to possession of the site, or would be so entitled but for the rights of any persons, to station mobile homes on land forming part of the site.

The expression "occupier" is defined differently, however, and this divergence sharply distinguishes the categories of

---

[9] *R. v. Glossop Union* (1866) L.R. 1 Q.B. 227.
[10] *Levene v. I.R.C.* [1928] A.C. 217.

persons entitled to protection under the two Acts.

The 1968 Act, by section 1(1), defines the occupier as the person who is entitled to a residential contract.

The term "occupier" is not directly defined in the 1983 Act at all. Instead, section 1(1) thereof provides an indirect definition by stipulating that the Act applies to agreements whereby a person ("the occupier") is entitled both to station a mobile home on land forming part of a protected site and to occupy that home as his only or main residence.

Two points of difference appear to mark the position of an occupier under the Acts. They are:

(1) Under the 1983 Act, the occupier must own the caravan in which he is living. This is, it is submitted, necessarily implied in the requirement that the occupier is entitled to station the structure on site. A mere lessee cannot be so entitled. By contrast, as has been seen, the lessee of a mobile home or caravan is protected under the 1968 Act by being entitled to occupy as his residence a caravan which is stationed on a protected site.[11]

(2) The concept of residence is more strictly circumscribed under the 1983 Act. Two residences of equal importance would not qualify whereas, it seems, under the 1968 Act they would.

---

[11] For a fuller discussion of the differences between owning and renting a caravan or mobile home, see above, p. 87.

Chapter 10

THE RIGHTS OF OWNERS AND OCCUPIERS UNDER THE 1968 ACT

General

Although the Caravan Sites Act 1968 has, to a large extent, been supplemented by the Mobile Homes Act 1983, the restrictions on eviction and harassment contained in Part I of the 1968 Act are still of importance.

It will, in particular, be appropriate to have recourse to the Act in the following circumstances:

(1) Where an occupier is not protected under the 1983 Act. This will occur, predominantly, in the case of residential occupiers who do not own the caravan or mobile home in which they are living but are leasing it from, say, the site operator.[1]

(2) Where an occupier is protected under the 1983 Act but does not enjoy, under his agreement, a right to quiet enjoyment.[2] In such cases, the residual statutory protection against eviction and harassment may be of considerable importance.

(3) Whether or not an occupier is protected under the 1983 Act, the provisions of the 1968 Act regulating the obtaining and suspension of eviction orders will apply.[3]

Minimum Length of Notice

The meaning of the term "residential contract" has already

---

[1] Another example is gypsies occupying local authority accommodation; see p. 96.

[2] Such a term may be, but is not necessarily, implied by the court; see 1983 Act, Sch. I Part II clause 1.

[3] Because, it seems, all agreements under the 1983 Act must be "residential contracts" under the 1968 Act as well.

been considered.[4] Section 2 of the 1968 Act provides that, in any case where a residential contract is determinable by notice given by either party to the other, such notice shall be invalid unless it is given not less than four weeks before the date on which it is to take effect.[5]

The form of notice is subject to the terms of the residential contract. There is nothing in the Act that requires it to be in writing. However, in cases where the contract is silent on the point, it is a sensible precaution for the site owner to ensure that notice is given in writing (and keep a copy) so as to avoid the evidential difficulty of proving proper notice if it is subsequently disputed.

It seems unlikely that notice will be required where a site owner terminates a licence or contract because the land is being used without a site licence in contravention of section 1(1) of the 1960 Act.[6]

Similarly, where an occupier is protected by having an agreement to which the 1983 Act applies, it is submitted that there is no requirement on the site owner to serve notice under the 1968 Act. The reasons for this are not entirely straightforward and will be considered in the next chapter.

Protection Against Eviction

Section 3(1) of the 1968 Act creates two offences, which may be prosecuted by the local authority,[7] in relation to the wrongful eviction of a residential occupier.

For the purpose of the section, the term "occupier" is, by section 3(2), expressed to include a widow or widower of the original occupier who was residing with the deceased at the time of death.[8]

---

[4] See p. 96.
[5] This period includes the first and excludes the last day; see *Schnabel v. Allard* [1967] 1 Q.B. 627.
[6] See p. 108.
[7] 1968 Act, s. 14(2).
[8] [2002] 4 All E.R. 1162.

It is submitted that the words "widow" and "widower" must now be interpreted to include a same-sex partner, following the decision of the Court of Appeal in *Mendoza v. Ghaidan*, a case decided on the Rent Act 1977. In that case, the secure tenant of residential premises (i.e. with security of tenure under the 1977 Act) died. His same-sex partner claimed to succeed to the tenancy under paragraph 2 of Schedule 1 to the 1977 Act as a person living with the original tenant as his husband. The Court upheld the claim on the following grounds. Paragraph 2 of Schedule 1 to the 1977 Act allows "spouses" and "persons living with the original tenant as his or her husband or wife" to succeed to a secure tenancy. Article 14 of the European Convention on Human Rights (enacted in the Human Rights Act 1998) provides that the enjoyment of the rights and freedoms of the Convention shall be secured without discrimination on any ground such as sex, race, colour, language, religion, political or other opinion, national or social origin, association with a national minority, property, birth or other status. Article 8 puts the state under an obligation to take action to protect the values of private and family life and the home. In this instance, same-sex and heterosexual couples were treated differently in relation to the home. There was no adequate justification for the difference in treatment. It was thus necessary to read the legislation in such a way as to give effect to the convention rights of same-sex partners.

Whilst the words used in the 1968 Act are "widow" and "widower", it is submitted that these words now have to be interpreted in the light of the *Mendoza* case so as to include same-sex partners.

If there is no person residing with the occupier at his or her death, then any member of the original occupier's family will qualify for protection provided they satisfy the residence test as set out above. There is no precise definition of "family" in the context of the 1968 Act. It is likely that the courts will interpret the word in the same way as it has been interpreted in the relation to the 1977 Act, in the light of the *Mendoza* case and any other cases which may arise out of the Human Rights Act 1998.

Thus:

(1) Anyone who is a relative will, provided that the relationship is not too distant,[9] be held to be a member of the occupier's family.

(2) A same-sex partner who does not qualify as a widow or a widower in accordance with the decision in the *Mendoza* case may, depending on the stability of the relationship, also be a member of the family. It is difficult to envisage circumstances where a surviving same-sex partner would not be treated as a widow or a widower, but the law relating to human rights is of recent origin and is developing rapidly.[10]

(1) The Offences
A person is guilty of an offence under the section if:

(i) during the subsistence of a residential contract, he unlawfully deprives the occupier of his occupation on the protected site of any caravan which the occupier is entitled by the contract to station and occupy as his residence on site;

(ii) after the expiration or termination of a residential contract, he enforces, otherwise than by proceedings in the court, any right to exclude the occupier from the protected site or from any such caravan, or to remove or exclude a caravan from the site.

It should be observed that a body corporate is capable of committing an offence relating to wrongful eviction.[11] Where a body corporate does commit such an offence,

---

[9] See, e.g. *Brock v. Wollams* [1949] 2 K.B. 388.
[10] *Mendoza v. Ghaidan* [2002] 4 All E.R. 1162.
[11] i.e. from the principle that a body corporate is a legal person.

and the offence is proved to have been committed with the consent or connivance of, or through the neglect of, an official or purported official thereof, such person is, by virtue of section 14(1) of the Act, also guilty of the offence.

It will be seen that the object of the offences created by section 3(1) is to prevent an occupier from being evicted without a court order. For the purpose of the Act, the expression "the court" means the county court.[12]

(2) Statutory Defence

A statutory defence is contained in section 3(4) of the Act. It applies only to offences relating to wrongful eviction.[13] It is there provided that it shall be a defence for an accused person to prove that he believed, and had reasonable cause to believe, that the occupier of the caravan had ceased to reside on the site.

As in the case of many statutory defences, the burden of proof is on the accused. That burden is not as heavy as ordinarily rests on the prosecution. It will be sufficient if the accused can satisfy a court on what is often termed the balance of probability.[14]

It is important to realise that there are two aspects to the defence. What a person believes is a subjective matter. The question of what amounts to reasonable cause for a particular belief is an objective criterion and is answered by the test of what a reasonable man would have believed in the circumstances. The sort of situation in which the defence may often be appropriate is where a caravan is removed from the site because it gives all the appearance of having been abandoned.

(3) Penalty

A person guilty of an offence relating to wrongful eviction is, on summary conviction, liable to a fine not exceeding

---

[12] 1968 Act, s. 5(1).
[13] *Cf.* the offence of harassment; see p. 104.
[14] *R. v. Carr-Briant* [1943] K.B. 607.

Level 5 on the standard scale (currently £5,000) or to imprisonment for a term not exceeding six months or to both.

This penalty does not affect the right of an occupier to take civil proceedings.[15] A conviction may, indeed, be persuasive evidence in such proceedings.

Protection Against Harassment

There is also provision under section 3(1) of the 1968 Act for the protection of residential occupiers against harassment. The protection afforded is substantially the same as that available in the case of wrongful eviction.

Section 3(1) makes it an offence for a person, whether during the subsistence or after the expiration or determination of a residential contract, to do certain acts with intent to cause the occupier either:

(i)   to abandon the occupation of the caravan or remove it from the site; or

(ii) to refrain from exercising any right or pursuing any remedy in respect thereof.

The acts prohibited by the section fall into two classes. They consist of:

(1) Acts calculated to interfere with the peace or comfort of the occupier or persons residing with him.

(2) Acts involving the persistent withdrawal or withholding of services or facilities reasonably required for the occupation of the caravan as a residence on the site.

There is no statutory defence, as in the case of an offence of wrongful eviction, but it is apparent that intention is the essence of the offence. Intention is not an easy matter to prove and the burden of proving it rests with the

---

[15]   1968 Act, s. 3(3).

prosecution. In many cases, of course, the acts themselves will be strong evidence of the intention behind them, but it will not always be so. Where a site owner raises an alternative explanation, and is believed, as to the reasons for his actions, he must be acquitted of the offence of harassment.

Apart from the difference in the nature of the defences available, the offence of harassment is subject to the same statutory provisions as the offences of wrongful eviction. Thus:

(i)   the term "occupier" extends to the widow or widower, etc. of the original occupier (s.3(2));

(ii) the same statutory penalties apply (s.3(3));

(iii) a body corporate and its officials may be guilty of the offence (s.14(1));

(iv) the local authority may institute proceedings for the offence (s.14(2)).

Obtaining an Eviction Order

Where the owner of a protected site is entitled to possession, after the expiration or termination of a residential contract, he may apply to the county court for an eviction order. The provisions in the 1968 Act for the obtaining and suspension of eviction orders will be relevant in cases where the occupier is protected under the 1983 Act as well as in cases where his protection is limited to that afforded under the 1968 Act.

Under section 21 of the County Courts Act 1984, the local county court has jurisdiction in actions for the recovery of possession of land. Court proceedings are generally governed by Part 55 of the Civil Procedure Rules 1998 (as amended).

Proceedings should be started in the county court for the district in which the caravan is situated by means of a summons for a fixed date action, together with the particulars of claim and copies for all the parties to the action. The summons may be prepared by the claimant and served by him on the defendant(s). The particulars of claim must:

(i)   identify the land sought to be recovered;

(ii) state whether the claim relates to residential property;

(iii) give full details of the tenancy or agreement under which the land is held;

(iv) state the grounds on which possession is claimed;

(v)   give details of the person(s) in possession of the land.

The Civil Procedure Rules 1998 (as amended) and Practice Directions prescribe the details of the procedures which must be followed after the summons has been issued and served on the defendant(s).

The court will fix the date for the hearing of the claim. At the hearing, the claimant must prove his case and, if satisfied that the case has been made out, the judge or district judge will make an order for possession. The order is enforced by a warrant of possession and can, if necessary, be executed by the court bailiff.

The foregoing is only a brief summary of the procedure for recovering possession. A full description of the procedure is outside the scope of this book.

Where a site owner is seeking to terminate an agreement under the 1983 Act, it will still be necessary to seek an eviction order from the court.[16]

Provision for Suspension of Eviction Orders

By virtue of section 4(1) of the 1968 Act, where a court makes an eviction order it may suspend its enforcement

---

[16]   i.e. the county court.

for such period not exceeding twelve months as it thinks reasonable. In suspending an order, the court may impose such conditions as it thinks reasonable, including conditions as to the payment of rent or other periodical payments, or of arrears of such rent or payments.[17] In general, where an order is suspended, no order for costs should be made unless the court feels that the conduct of one of the parties provides special reasons for doing so.[18] An order that is suspended may be varied as to either length or conditions imposed on the application of either party but it cannot be extended for more than twelve months at a time.[19]

A caravan dweller cannot expect to have an order suspended as of right. Section 4(4) lays down certain criteria that must be applied before an order relating to the conduct of the occupier is suspended. The court is directed to have regard to all the circumstances of the case and, in particular, to:

(1) Whether the occupier has failed, before or after the expiration or termination of a residential contract, to observe any terms or conditions of the contract, any conditions of the site licence, or any reasonable rules made by the owner for the management and conduct of the site or the maintenance of caravans on the site.

(2) Whether the occupier has unreasonably refused an offer by the owner to renew the residential contract or make another such contract for a reasonable period and on reasonable terms.

(3) Whether the occupier has failed to make reasonable efforts to obtain other suitable accommodation for his caravan elsewhere (or, as the case may be, another suitable caravan and accommodation for it).

---

[17] 1968 Act, s. 4(2).
[18] 1968 Act, s. 4(5).
[19] 1968 Act, s. 4(3).

The court has no power to suspend an order under the provisions of the 1968 Act where:

(1) The proceedings are taken by a local authority in respect of a site leased or managed by them.[20]

(2) There is no site licence in force in respect of the site.[21] In this context, it should be observed that an order cannot be suspended beyond the expiration of a current site licence.

Quite apart from its suspension powers under section 4, the court has a certain limited jurisdiction to postpone the operation of its own orders.[22] It may perhaps be argued, therefore, that in certain circumstances the court could use its own inherent jurisdiction to suspend an order for possession even where it would fall outside the ambit of the 1968 Act. Such cases are, in practice, likely to be extremely rare.

Land Used Without a Site Licence

It will be remembered that under the Caravan Sites and Control of Development Act 1960, by virtue of section 12(1), the occupier, as defined by the Act,[23] was enabled to take possession of the land and terminate a licence or tenancy where land was being used as a caravan site without there being a current site licence in force.

Section 5(4) of the 1968 Act expressly preserves that right "subject to the foregoing provisions" of the Act. The implications of that proviso are not immediately obvious. It seems apparent that a residential occupant would be entitled to be protected against wrongful eviction and harassment even where he was using land without a current site licence.

---

[20] 1960 Act, s. 24; see ch. 7.
[21] 1968 Act, s. 4(6).
[22] Housing Act 1980, s. 89.
[23] See ch. 3.

On the other hand, it is equally apparent that, in such circumstances, the court would have no power to suspend the operation of an order for possession.[24] Nor is it likely that the residential occupant could require at least four weeks' notice to be served upon him under section 2. Section 2 only applies where a licence or contract is determinable by notice. The act of taking possession and terminating under the 1960 Act does not appear to contemplate the giving of notice at all.

Compulsory Purchase

The provisions of the 1968 Act do not extend to compulsory purchase. In particular, an authority entitled to take possession of land by virtue of powers under the Compulsory Purchase Act 1965 may issue a warrant of possession and the court has no power to entertain an application for suspension.[25]

It is not possible in a book of this character to examine any of the detailed law relating to compulsory purchase. It is, however, worth noting that the Land Compensation Act 1973 affords rights to persons displaced from dwellings by compulsory acquisition.

By virtue of section 29 of the 1973 Act, persons so displaced are entitled, in certain circumstances, to claim payments known as "home loss payments". Section 39 imposes a duty on the relevant authorities to re-house such persons. The Act is specifically expressed to apply to caravan dwellers.[26]

---

[24] i.e. by virtue of s. 4(6)(b) of the 1968 Act.
[25] 1968 Act, s. 5(3).
[26] Land Compensation Act 1973, ss. 33 and 40.

Chapter 11

THE MOBILE HOMES ACT 1983

Background

Notwithstanding the passing of the 1960 and 1968 Acts, the protection afforded to the permanent caravan dweller was effectively limited. In particular, the Acts were silent on such important matters as leases, site charges, and arbitration about rent and resale. Indeed, the House of Lords had held in the case of *Chertsey U.D.C. v. Mixnam's Properties*[1] that such matters fell outside the scope of site licence control and were contrary to the intention of the 1960 Act.

This placed residents of mobile homes in an especially difficult position. As was pointed out in Parliament, although they were home owners, they were tenants of the sites on which those homes stood. They were also outside any rent control or any landlord and tenant legislation.

The Mobile Homes Act 1975, which came into effect on the 1st October 1975, was designed to meet these anomalies. Its general purpose was to provide certain rights and responsibilities between site owner and occupier. It achieved this by means of compulsory written agreements containing detailed terms and a right of recourse to the court should disputes arise.

In the event, what had, in any case, only been intended as a temporary piece of legislation proved to be seriously deficient in ensuring that protection granted was actually enjoyed.

The most important defect was, undoubtedly, that in most instances the occupier had only a limited time in which to seek the benefit of a written agreement. The burden of

---
[1]   [1964] 2 All E.R. 627; 15 P. & C.R. 331; see ch. 5.

110

seeking it lay on him and notice, in writing, of intention to occupy was required. Most occupiers were unaware, in time, of their legal rights. By the time they discovered them, it was often too late.

There were other problems. For example, under the 1975 Act an occupier wishing to sell his home was obliged to offer it, first, to the site owner at a fair market price. An unscrupulous owner could, if he were so minded, force sales at seriously depressed prices.

The Mobile Homes Review, which was set up, *inter alia*, to monitor the effectiveness of the 1975 Act, concluded that it was not based on a full consideration of the problems which can arise over time. A serious flaw was to leave the occupier vulnerable to a change of policy on the part of the existing site owner.

The Mobile Homes Act 1983 represents an attempt to remedy the glaring defects of its predecessor. At the same time, it seeks to strike a balance between the legitimate claims and expectations of the site owner as well as the occupier. It does this in a wholly original way by implying an agreement between site owner and occupier as soon as the latter agrees to come onto the site.

Agreements to Which the Act Applies

Section 1(1) of the 1983 Act provides that the Act shall apply to any agreement under which a person is entitled to station a mobile home on land forming part of a protected site[2] and to occupy it as his only or main residence.

From that basic statement, a number of important consequences ensue. It is apparent that the Act extends, almost exclusively, to persons who are residential owner-occupiers of their mobile homes. A confusing feature is that the Act does not actually state this. It is, however, necessarily implied from the above requirement because

---

[2] See ch. 9.

(in almost every case) the only person entitled to station the mobile home on site will be the owner. A person who merely leases the structure (as opposed to the pitch) will, ordinarily, not himself be entitled to station the mobile home on the site and so will not be entitled to protection under the 1983 Act.[3]

The Act applies to "any" agreement so that it covers such agreement whenever it was concluded and, in particular, irrespective of whether or not it was concluded before the 1983 Act came into force (on 20th May 1983).

The exact status of the occupier's interest is irrelevant. Whether he holds the site under an oral agreement, a long leasehold interest, a 1975 Act agreement or anything else, the site owner must comply with the provisions of the 1983 Act so long as the conditions laid down in section 1(1) are satisfied. It should be understood that it is the entitlement rather than the fact of residential occupation that marks the starting point of the protection.[4] An agreement originally outside the ambit of the 1983 Act may be varied so as to become an agreement to which the Act applies. In those circumstances, the Act will apply as from the date of such variation.[5]

It may not always be easy to determine whether an occupier is entitled to, or does, occupy the mobile home as his only or main residence. This is, primarily, a question of fact. Intention and practical possibility of residence are important factors.[6] It is clear that an involuntary and temporary absence will not break the thread of causation.[7]

---

[3]   However, apart from the 1968 Act, he may be protected under the legislation relating to the statutory control of residential tenancies; see ch. 12.
[4]   The date of the agreement may be all important in determining the site operator's obligations; see below.
[5]   1983 Act, s. 1(4).
[6]   *Omar Parks Ltd. v. Elkington* [1993] 1 All E.R. 282.
[7]   *Morrison Holdings Ltd. v. Manders Property (Wolverhampton) Ltd.* [1976] 2 All E.R. 205; [1976] 1 W.L.R. 533, C.A.; and see generally *Brown v. Brash* [1948] 2 K.B. 247.

It is emphasised, again, that although the expression "mobile home" is used throughout the 1983 Act, it has the same meaning as the term "caravan" under the 1960 Act, as amended by the 1968 Act.[8]

The Written Statement

Once it is established that there is an agreement to which the 1983 Act applies, the site owner[9] is under a duty to give[10] the occupier of the mobile home a written statement by virtue of section 1(2) thereof.

By the same section, the statement must contain the following particulars:

(a) the names and addresses of the parties and the date of commencement;

(b) a description of the land on which the occupier is entitled to station the mobile home sufficient to identify it;

(c) the express terms of the agreement;

(d) the terms that are implied under section 2(1) and Part I of Schedule 1 to the Act (see below).

In addition, section 1(2) requires the statement to comply with any regulations made by the Secretary of State pursuant to section 1(6) of the Act.

Regulations have been made coincident with the entry into force of the 1983 Act.[11] They prescribe that the written statement shall be in a certain form as set out in the Schedule to the regulations.[12] Additional particulars

---

[8] See above, p. 95.

[9] See ch. 9.

[10] The statement may, of course, be sent to the occupier. Perhaps "serve" or "provide" would have been better in this context.

[11] The Mobile Homes (Written Statement) Regulations 1983, S.I. 1983 No. 1749.

[12] The Schedule is reproduced in Appendix C. The statement may be in a form "substantially to the like effect". In practice, it is unwise to deviate from the standard form.

contained in the form are the date of commencement of the agreement between site owner and occupier and the date on which the site owner's interest or estate in the land and planning permission for the site will end. As well as this, the statement must include information for the occupier setting out, in simple form, all his rights under the new Act.

The site owner must give the occupier his written statement within three months of concluding an agreement with the occupier.[13] Where, however, the agreement was made before 20th May 1983, the site owner had, under section 1(3), six months from 20th May to comply with his statutory obligation. The occupier may, in the event of failure to comply, apply to the court for an order requiring the owner to provide the statement.[14]

Not all the implications of the requirement of the written statement are immediately obvious. They may be summarised as follows:

(1) The statement is merely evidence of the agreement between the parties. The actual agreement will, in the majority of cases, have been concluded at an earlier date. The agreement will be binding on the parties as soon as it is made so that failure on the part of the site owner to serve the written statement does not leave the occupier unprotected. In particular, all the terms automatically implied under the 1983 Act will apply as soon as the agreement is made. However, it does appear that the court cannot imply terms under Part II of Schedule I (see below) or vary or delete any express term unless and until a written statement has been served.[15]

---

[13]   1983 Act, s. 1(2).
[14]   1983 Act, s. 1(5). The application can, it seems, be made at any time and can be made against a successor in title to the original owner; see p. 125.
[15]   This seems to follow from the wording of s. 2(2) and (3) and is probably an unintended anomaly; see p. 125.

(2) Because the statement will contain all the intended terms of the agreement, there will usually not be any need for a formal written agreement between the parties. In one instance, however, there may be. Where the court, under section 2, implies certain additional terms or alters existing terms (see below), there appears to be no provision in the 1983 Act for any new written statement or formal alteration of the statement already supplied.[16] In some cases, therefore, the occupier's agreement may be an untidy amalgam of written statement and subsequent court order. In such circumstances, it may still be prudent to set out all the terms in revised written form.

(3) There is no immediate sanction on an owner who fails to provide a written statement. If, however, on an application by the occupier, the court makes an order that he does so he would be in contempt by failing to comply.

Duration of the Agreement

Where an occupier has an agreement to which the 1983 Act applies, his right to station the mobile home on site will subsist indefinitely unless:

(i) the agreement is terminated by either occupier or site owner in accordance with the provisions of the Act (for which see below); or

(ii) the site owner's interest or estate is insufficient to enable him to grant the right for an indefinite period or else his planning permission to use the protected site as a site for mobile homes expires at the end of a specified period.[17]

In cases under (i), the right will expire when the agreement is validly terminated. Alternatively, the right will not

---

[16] It may be that the court could make such a consequential order by virtue of s. 2(4); see p. 125.
[17] 1983 Act, Sch. I Part I at paras. 1, 2(1) and 2(2).

subsist, under (ii), beyond the expiry of the owner's interest, estate or planning permission.[18] It should, however, be observed that a change of circumstances, whereby the limitation on the site owner's interest, etc. is extended, will operate so as to extend the occupier's right to station his home on site for the same period.[19]

Unfortunately, the provisions as to duration appear to afford considerable scope for evasion on the part of the site owner. The grant of a short lease by the site owner to, say, his wife would seem to be all that is required to avoid the statutory commitment altogether. The wife would be the party to the agreement with the occupier and the occupier's right to station the home on site would terminate on expiration of her lease. The site owner on resuming control of the site could then simply refuse to conclude any further agreement with the occupier, thereby divesting him of any protection whatever under either the 1968 or 1983 Acts.

The duration provisions are terms automatically implied into every agreement. Thus they take effect notwithstanding any contrary express term.[20]

Content of the Agreement

(1) Express Terms

The general principle is that parties are free to insert any express terms into the agreement provided that such terms do not purport to conflict with terms automatically implied under the 1983 Act.[21]

It follows that the parties may agree, as express terms, provisions that alter or vary those terms that a court may imply, on application, under Part II of Schedule I to the 1983 Act. In addition, there may be special stipulations

---

[18]   1983 Act, Sch. I Part I at paras. 2(1) and 2(2).
[19]   1983 Act, Sch. I Part I at para. 2(3).
[20]   1983 Act, s. 2(1).
[21]   This follows from s. 2(1) of the 1983 Act.

that the site owner and occupier want in the agreement that have nothing to do with anything contained in the Act.

In practice, and assuming that there is no dispute, the usual express terms will relate to those matters concerning which terms may be implied by the court under Part II of Schedule I. These cover:

(a) the right of the occupier to quiet enjoyment;

(b) the sums payable by the occupier and the times of payment;

(c) the review, at annual intervals, of the sums so payable;

(d) the provision or improvement of services available on site and the use by the occupier of such services;

(e) the preservation of the amenity of the site;

(f) the maintenance and repair of the site by the owner;

(g) the maintenance and repair of the mobile home by the occupier;

(h) access by the owner to the land on which the mobile home is sited.

From the occupier's point of view, negotiations over express terms should take place before the written statement is served. By arranging matters in that way, there will be less pressure to agree to unsuitable provisions and more time for careful consideration of exactly what is being offered. It is submitted that, in most cases, written statements will not be served unless the parties have agreed all the express terms or it is clear that negotiations have broken down. In the absence of agreement, the service of a written statement smacks of a certain unilateralism on the part of a site owner. It should be borne in mind that, once the statement is served, the occupier has only six months to apply for revision of its terms.[22]

The 1983 Act contains a number of dangers for unwary occupiers. In particular, when undertaking negotiations with the site owner, efforts should be made to ensure that there is express provision for control over pitch fees. Whilst it may be possible to persuade a court to include such a term on an application under section 2,[23] this is by no means a foregone conclusion. Certainly there is no such term in the Act itself.

Care should be taken by both sides to include terms dealing with all the matters set out in Part II of Schedule I. In that respect, the 1983 Act is less secure than its predecessor where these matters had to be dealt with. If something is omitted, it seems doubtful from the way that the Act is phrased that an owner or occupier can assume that such a term is implied, in any event, at common law. Once six months have expired following service of the written statement, that is an end of the matter. Thus terms as to, for example, quiet enjoyment or site maintenance and repair will be lost for ever.[24] This is hardly satisfactory and one questions whether it can have been the intention of the legislature to leave parties potentially unprotected in this way.

Finally, attention should be directed at the outset to the nature of the court to which it is desired to submit disputes. Under the Act, disputes can be submitted either to the county court or to an arbitrator where the parties have agreed, in writing, to submit disputes to arbitration.[25] There may be serious disadvantage to occupiers, in

---

[22]   See p. 125.
[23]   The arguments are difficult and depend upon a liberal interpretation of s. 2(3) and (4); see p. 126.
[24]   There might, of course, be potential actions against the other party in tort or specific enactment such as the Occupier's Liability Act 1957.
[25]   1983 Act, s. 5(1) and see p. 127. The arbitration is governed by the Arbitration Act 1996.

particular, in agreeing to submit disputes to arbitration (for which see below), and much may depend on the particular relationships between the parties. It seems desirable that the type of forum in which disputes will be litigated should be clarified by way of express term in the written statement.

(2) Implied Terms

By this is meant the terms automatically implied into every agreement under Part I of Schedule I to the Act. It should not be confused with those terms that a court may imply under Part II of Schedule I (see above) which will, in most cases, usually be included as express terms.

The important point to appreciate is that terms which are automatically implied cannot be altered and take effect despite any inconsistent express term in the agreement.[26]

All these terms are set out in Part II (the information section) of the written statement[27] and there will be no need to set them out again in the section dealing with express terms because they are invariable.

The terms implied are as follows:

(a) *Duration of the agreement* (1983 Act, Part I of Schedule I, paras. 1 and 2). These have already been considered (see above).

(b) *Termination by either occupier or owner* (*ibid* at paras. 3-6). These are considered, in more detail, below.

(c) *Recovery of overpayments by occupier* (*ibid* at para. 7). This permits an occupier, on termination, to recover any payments made in respect of a period beginning after the termination.

(d) *Sale of the mobile home* (*ibid* at para. 8). The automatic provisions as to sale enable an occupier to sell his

---

26 1983 Act, s. 2(1).
27 See Appendix C.

mobile home on site and to assign the agreement to a
person approved of by the owner. The owner's approval
must not be unreasonably withheld.[28] Where such sale
occurs, the owner is entitled to a commission up to a
rate currently not in excess of ten per cent.[29]

(e) *Gift of the mobile home (ibid* at para. 9). Similar provisions
enable the occupier to give the mobile home, and to
assign the agreement, to a member of his family[30]
approved by the owner. Again, the owner's approval
must not be unreasonably withheld. In this instance,
no commission is payable to the site owner.

(f) *Re-siting of the mobile home (ibid* at para. 10). Where the
agreement contains a term (e.g. as to reasonable
access to the occupier's pitch for site maintenance)
that entitles the owner temporarily to resite the mobile
home on a different site, it is automatically implied
that such alternative site will be broadly comparable to
the original site, and also that all costs and expenses
incurred in consequence of the re-siting shall be paid
by the site owner.

All the automatically implied terms take effect as soon as
an agreement is made between the site owner and occupier.
They are not, in any sense, dependent on the written
statement or on the result of negotiations between the
parties. Therefore, once the agreement is concluded, it is
very much in the site owner's interest to agree express
terms as to pitch fees, mobile home maintenance, etc.
because the occupier has an indefinite right to station his

---

[28] Presumably this test is an analogous principle to the case law on s.
19(1)(a) of the Landlord and Tenant Act 1927.

[29] See the Mobile Homes (Commissions) Order 1983, S.I. 1983 No. 748.

[30] This seems to cover a wife or husband, parent, grandparent, child,
grandchild, brother, sister, uncle, aunt, nephew or niece as well as any
such relation by marriage or half blood. Stepchildren, adopted children
and illegitimate children are also included as well as people living
together as husband and wife. See 1983 Act, s. 5(3) and compare the
position under the 1968 Act, above at p. 100.

mobile home on the pitch as soon as he is permitted to come onto the site. That essential right subsists despite the fact that other vitally important terms may not have been agreed upon.

Termination Provisions

The provisions as to termination of agreements are automatically implied under Part I of Schedule I to the 1983 Act. As such they cannot be varied and do not fall to be recited in the main body of the written statement (see above).

The occupier may terminate an agreement provided that he gives to the owner notice of termination in writing not less than four weeks before the date on which it is to take effect.[31] No specific form is necessary but care must be taken to prevent the notice being declared invalid by failing to give the requisite period of notice.[32] It is to be observed that an occupier may terminate in this way even if his agreement is for a fixed term with time still to run thereunder.

The position of the site owner is more complicated. He may only terminate if he obtains the court's approval under one or more of a number of specified grounds. These are set out at paragraphs 4, 5 and 6 of Part I of Schedule I which provide that an owner shall be entitled to terminate the agreement forthwith if, on his application, the court[33] is satisfied that:

(a) the occupier has broken a term of the agreement and has failed, within a reasonable time, to comply with a notice to remedy the breach. The court must also consider, under this head, that it is reasonable for the agreement to be terminated; or

---

[31] 1983 Act, Sch. I Part I at para. 3.
[32] See *Schnabel v. Allard* [1967] 1 Q.B. 627; [1966] 3 All E.R. 816.
[33] Including, if agreed, an arbitrator.

(b) the occupier is not occupying the mobile home as his only or main residence; or

(c) having regard to its age and condition, the mobile home is either having a detrimental effect on the amenity of the site, or is likely to have such an effect within the next five years. The site owner may, under this head, make an initial application to terminate the agreement at the end of five years after commencement thereof and, thereafter, every succeeding five years.[34]

It is submitted that the burden of proving each of the above grounds lies upon the site owner.

Ground (a) is, perhaps, the most complex because three hurdles have to be overcome before termination is permitted. First, there must be a breach of one of the terms of the agreement. Then, a notice served by the owner requiring the occupier to remedy that breach must have been disregarded by the occupier (after a reasonable time has elapsed). Finally, the court must consider it reasonable to permit termination.

It is clear that the notice requiring the occupier to remedy the breach must be in writing.[35] The Act does not, however, prescribe any particular contents. Presumably, like a notice served under section 146 of the Law of Property Act 1925, notice served under the 1983 Act should specify the particular breach complained of and require the occupier to remedy it.[36] Not all breaches are capable of remedy but, as in the case of a section 146 notice, that probably does not avoid the necessity of written notice.

What is a reasonable time for compliance will depend

---

[34] 1983 Act, Sch. I Part I at para. 6(2) defines the "relevant period" as "the period of five years beginning with the commencement of the agreement and each succeeding period of five years".

[35] It is, surely, artificial to speak of "serving" an oral notice; see 1983 Act, Sch. I Part I para. 4(1).

[36] There are, however, significant differences with a s. 146 notice and the analogy cannot be pressed too far.

upon all the circumstances of the case and, in particular, the nature of the breach. In practice, the court's decision on this is likely to be exercised on principles analogous to those in section 146 cases. Similarly, it is submitted that, in deciding whether or not it is reasonable to permit termination, the court will adopt similar criteria to those used in case law under section 98 of the Rent Act 1977 (in relation to regulated tenancies) and section 9 of the Housing Act 1988 (in relation to assured tenancies).

Owners seeking to establish a right to terminate under grounds (b) and (c) above must satisfy the court as to certain factual matters. Once the grounds are established, the court must permit termination and has no residual discretion as to reasonableness.

Whether an occupier is using the mobile home as his residence is not merely a question of whether he is, at the time of application, currently in actual occupation. Temporary absence does not break the thread of residential occupation.

It is submitted that, under ground (c), it is the condition of the mobile home that will be the predominant factor in deciding whether to permit the owner to terminate the agreement. Although paragraph 6 enjoins the court to have regard to both age and condition, it is obviously possible to have an old mobile home that is perfectly capable of lasting another five years. By contrast, a new home may deteriorate rapidly if subjected to harsh treatment. It seems unlikely that a mobile home will be held to threaten site amenity merely because of its age whereas it might well do so by virtue of its condition.

Once the site owner has established a right to terminate, he may do so forthwith. The court cannot restrict that entitlement in any way.

The manner in which termination should be effected in these circumstances is not, however, clear. It will be recalled that the 1968 Act regulates the termination of residential contracts which are "determinable by notice" by stipulating that such notice must be at least four weeks before the date on which it is to take effect.[37] Agreements to which the 1983 Act applies are not, so far as the site owner is concerned, determinable by notice because they may be terminated "forthwith". It is submitted, therefore, that the requirements of the 1968 Act do not apply to site owners entitled to terminate under a court order in this context.[38]

Having validly terminated the agreement, it will still be necessary for a site owner to obtain an eviction order from the county court under the 1968 Act. Indeed, failure to do so would be an offence under section 3(1) of that Act.

Where the application to terminate has been made to the county court, there seems to be no reason, in principle, why the application for an eviction order should not be brought at the same time. When that court permits termination, it can be effected, without notice, in the same proceedings and an eviction order may then be made. Such order can, of course, be suspended on the same conditions and using the same criteria as under the 1968 Act.[39]

Procedural difficulties will arise in cases where an arbitrator hears and approves the application by the site owner for termination. An arbitrator cannot make an eviction order under the 1968 Act. It will, therefore, be necessary for the owner to take out a separate application before the county court after termination. This will involve extra costs and an unnecessary waste of time. It is another reason why care should be taken before deciding to resort to arbitration under section 5 of the 1983 Act.

---

[37] 1968 Act, s. 2; see above, p. 100.
[38] Insofar as the requirements apply to termination by an occupier, they are repeated in Part I of Sch. I to the 1983 Act at para. 3; see above, p. 121.
[39] See above, p. 106.

Claims for possession under the 1983 Act are generally governed by Part 55 of the Civil Procedure Rules 1998 (as amended), the detailed provisions of which are outside the scope of this book.

The Resolution of Disputes

From the foregoing it is apparent that disputes may arise between the parties in a number of different ways. They can be summarised as follows:

(1) An application by the site owner to bring an agreement with the occupier to an end (1983 Act, Part I of Schedule I at paras. 4, 5 and 6).

This has been dealt with in the previous section.

(2) An application by the occupier requiring the site owner to serve a written statement upon him (1983 Act, s. 1(5)).

Such application may be made at any time. In many cases it will be sensible to delay making it until it is quite clear that negotiations have broken down. The effect of a premature application will be to start time running against the occupier once the written statement has been served. Thereafter, he has only six months to dispute the terms of the agreement (see below).

(3) An application by either site owner or occupier asking the court to:

(i) imply additional terms under Part II of Schedule I to the 1983 Act and/or to vary or delete any express term of the agreement (1983 Act, s. 2(2) and (3));

(ii) settle any dispute that subsequently arises in relation to the operation of the agreement (1983 Act, s. 4).

Applications for the implication of additional terms or the variation or deletion of terms contained in the written statement must be made within six months of the service of the written statement.[40] If no application is made within that time, the parties are bound by the terms that are set out in the statement. It seems to follow that, unless and until the written statement has been served, no application can be entertained under section 2. On an application under section 2, the court shall, under section 2(4), make such provision as it considers just and equitable in the circumstances. It seems possible that the latter provision, taken in conjunction with the court's power to alter or vary express terms under section 2(3), may afford scope for arguing that the court can impose terms on the parties currently outside the ambit of the Act (e.g. as to ceiling limits for pitch fees).

Section 4 of the 1983 Act provides that the court has jurisdiction to determine any question arising under the Act or any agreement to which it applies. In addition, it has jurisdiction to entertain any proceedings brought under the Act or any such agreement.

The exact scope of this provision is uncertain. It certainly affords either party the opportunity of litigating factual disputes that may arise in relation to the agreement (e.g. as to whether owner or occupier is in breach of a particular term). It probably also allows either party to clarify their obligations in advance by seeking the court's direction on the extent of a provision in the agreement.

It is submitted, however, that section 4 does not permit unlimited applications. In particular, it does not provide either party with the opportunity to invite the court to imply terms into the agreement other than those set out in Schedule I. Nor does it give jurisdiction to waive time limits in respect of which particular applications must be made. The section is, however, so widely expressed that

---

[40]   1983 Act, s. 2(2) and (3).

there may be considerable scope for legal ingenuity in arguing its precise ambit.

For the purpose of the 1983 Act, the court is defined as meaning either:

(i) (in England and Wales) the county court for the district in which the protected site is situated; or

(ii) an arbitrator where the parties have agreed in writing to submit any question arising under the Act to arbitration or any agreement to which the Act applies to arbitration.[41]

If the proceedings are before the county court, the procedure for litigating disputes is governed by Part 55 of the Civil Procedure Rules 1998 (as amended) (see pages 105-106 above for a brief description).

The National Park Homes Council, Catherine House, Victoria Road, Aldershot, Hampshire GU11 1SS operates a voluntary conciliation scheme.

County Court or Arbitrator?

This is a difficult question and will depend upon the circumstances of each case. Site owners and occupiers should consider this problem at an early stage and, preferably, take legal advice on the point.

In general, there are significant dangers from an occupier's point of view in agreeing to arbitration. Civil legal aid will not be available for arbitration proceedings and it is, in consequence, important to determine whether an occupier would, in the event of dispute, qualify for legal aid. If he would, there seems little point in agreeing to an arbitration clause. Similarly, it is more expensive to enforce an arbitrator's decision in most instances. Sometimes a fresh action is necessary (e.g. where the arbitrator dies before

---

[41] 1983 Act, s. 5(1)(a).

completing the arbitration – section 26 of the Arbitration Act 1996); in other cases (e.g. failure on the part of the owner to comply with an order) any application for committal would have to be made to the Divisional Court.

Even from the site owner's perspective, there may be problems in appointing an arbitrator. The delay in obtaining an eviction order by having to make separate application to the county court has already been referred to. Other delays may occur. For example, the scope of any arbitration clause may be in dispute and have to be litigated before the county court in any event. The arbitrator will not always be legally qualified and may approach a case without sufficient regard to the nature of the evidence or the appropriate rules of law.

Having said that, arbitrations have certain advantages. An arbitrator often has greater familiarity with the practical problems involved. Sometimes it can be quicker and, in certain cases, less expensive.[42] The proceedings are usually less formal. There is finality, too, in that an arbitrator's decision on fact is normally not subject to appeal. This latter point is obviously a mixed blessing.

Solicitors and other advisers must weigh up all the different points in each case. Knowledge of the way in which a particular arbitrator is likely to approach the case may sometimes be the deciding factor.

Succession to an Agreement
(1) Successors of the Owner
Section 3(1) of the 1983 Act provides that an agreement to which the Act applies is binding on, and enures for the benefit of, any successor in title of the owner and any person claiming through or under the owner or his successor.

---

[42] This is not always so. In an arbitration, the parties are responsible for the arbitrator's remuneration and expenses.

This should not be confused with the situation that arises where an owner's interest or estate comes to an end. In that event, the occupier loses his rights to remain on site. It has already been seen that this represents one of the loopholes in the Act and may well be a source of abuse in the future.[43]

(2) Successors of the Occupier
Two possibilities are contemplated, namely:

(i) assignment;

(ii) death.

Where an agreement is lawfully assigned, section 3(2) of the Act provides that the agreement shall enure for the benefit of, and be binding on, the assignee.

Only the occupier can lawfully assign an agreement under the Act. Paragraph 9 of Part I of Schedule I permits him to do this in favour of a member of his family approved by the owner (see above). The assignee then becomes the occupier within the meaning of the Act.[44] Similarly, on sale the occupier may legitimately assign the agreement to a person approved by the owner (see above).

Where the occupier dies, the position is slightly more complicated. The relevant provisions are contained in section 3(3) and (4) of the Act and are, in summary, as follows:

(1) If the occupier dies leaving a widow or widower who was residing with them at death, then the benefit and burden of the agreement pass to that person.

(2) In the absence of a widow or widower, then the benefit and burden will pass to any member of the original occupier's family who are residing with them at the date of death.

---

[43] See p. 116.
[44] 1983 Act, s. 5(2).

(3) Where no relevant person or persons are residing with the occupier at death, the occupier will be succeeded by the person or persons entitled to the mobile home under his will or on intestacy. This is, however, subject to the following provisos:

(i)   such person will not be enabled, and cannot be required, to occupy the mobile home;

(ii) the site owner cannot terminate the agreement on the ground that the successor is not occupying the mobile home as his residence;

(iii) the successor may not give the mobile home and/ or assign the agreement to another member of the family.

This means, in practice, that the mobile home has to be sold if ownership passes by will or on intestacy to someone other than a person within (1) or (2) immediately above.

The wording of section 3(3) and (4) of the 1983 Act is effectively identical to that of section 3(2) of the 1968 Act in its reference to succession to a deceased occupier by the widow or widower of that person or by a member of that person's family. Accordingly, it is submitted that the ruling in the *Mendoza* case in relation to the Rent Act 1977 (see page 101 above) applies to the right of succession under the 1983 Act as it does to the right of succession under the 1968 Act.

A member of the family is defined as extending to a spouse, parent, grandparent, child, grandchild, brother, sister, uncle, aunt, nephew, or niece as well as any such relation by marriage or half blood. Stepchildren, adopted children and illegitimate children are also included as well as people living together as husband and wife.[45]

---

[45]   1983 Act, s. 5(3) and *cf.* the 1968 Act above at p. 101.

Powers of the Secretary of State

The Secretary of State has power to make a variety of orders in respect of protected sites and in respect of agreements to which the 1983 Act applies.

Residual powers available to the Secretary of State under the Mobile Homes Acts 1975 and 1983 are:

(1) To prescribe minimum standards with respect to the layout of, and the provision of facilities, services and equipment for, protected sites.[46]

(2) To prescribe particular requirements with which written statements under the 1983 Act must comply.[47]

(3) To specify rates of commission payable to the site owner on sale of the mobile home.[48]

All the above powers are exercisable by statutory instrument.

---

[46] 1975 Act, s. 7(1).
[47] 1983 Act, s. 1(2)(e); and see the Mobile Homes (Written Statement) Regulations 1983, S.I. 1983 No. 1749.
[48] 1983 Act, Sch. I Part I at para. 8(2); see the Mobile Homes (Commission) Order 1983, S.I. 1983 No. 748.

Chapter 12

STATUTORY CONTROL OVER RESIDENTIAL TENANCIES

Are Mobile Homes Protected?

As has been seen, the Mobile Homes Act 1983 does not apply to residential occupiers who rent the home in which they live as opposed to owning it. Whilst such persons enjoy a degree of protection against summary eviction from the pitch, under the 1968 Act, the question arises whether they may also be protected by the statutory controls over residential tenancies.

The principal statutory controls relating to residential tenancies are to be found in the Rent Act 1977 and the Housing Act 1988. Under both Acts, protection against eviction, some security of tenure and some control over the level of rents are provided for a person who has a tenancy of a dwelling-house which is let as a separate dwelling. In this context, a tenancy must be distinguished from a licence, since neither the 1977 nor the 1988 Acts apply to a dwelling which is occupied under a licence. As a general rule, a tenancy is created where there is a grant of exclusive possession of premises for a fixed or periodic term at a specified rent.[1] It is likely that the great majority of caravans and mobile homes let for residential purposes are subject to tenancies and not licences.

Can a caravan be a "dwelling-house" for the purposes of the 1977 and 1988 Acts? A stationary but moveable caravan has been held not to be a house.[2] However, a caravan which is let on a residential site and is not intended to be moved is almost certainly a dwelling within

---

[1] *Street v. Mountford* [1985] A.C. 809.
[2] *R. v. Rent Officer of the Nottinghamshire Registration Area ex parte Allen* [1985] 52 P. & C.R. 41.

the meaning of the Acts. In *R. v. Rent Officer of the Nottinghamshire Registration Area ex parte Allen*, the judge said:

> "Where a caravan is a movable chattel, there can be no question of its being properly described as a house. Where, on the other hand, it is rendered completely immobile by its being permanently blocked by some brick or concrete construction, then it is more likely to be regarded as a house ... If the occupancy of the caravan is such that it is plainly used by the tenant as his or her permanent home, then there is a greater likelihood of the caravan being permanently in place rather than being used as a temporary expedient."

Where a caravan was let as a separate dwelling before 15th January 1989, the tenancy was, as a general rule, regulated under the Rent Act 1977. Any such tenancy which still subsists remains subject to the 1977 Act and is known as a regulated tenancy. Where the letting was after 14th January 1989, the 1988 Act applies and the letting is known as an assured tenancy. A letting after 27th February 1997 is, with a few minor exceptions unlikely to be relevant to the letting of a caravan, an assured shorthold tenancy.

It is not possible in a book of this size to deal with individual provisions of the 1977 and 1988 Acts. If an owner or occupier is in doubt as to whether the Acts apply, they should consult one of the specialist textbooks on landlord and tenant law or, preferably, seek legal advice.

Part III

GYPSIES

Chapter 13
GYPSY SITES

The Provision of Gypsy Sites

By virtue of section 24(8) of the Caravan Sites and Control of Development Act 1960 (as amended by section 80 of the Criminal Justice and Public Order Act 1994), "gypsies" means "persons of nomadic habit of life, whatever their race or origin, but does not include members of an organised group of travelling showmen, or of persons engaged in travelling circuses, travelling together as such". The Court of Appeal has interpreted this to mean that "gypsies" are persons who wander or travel for the purpose of making or seeking their livelihood and they do not include persons who move from place to place without any connection between their movement and their means of livelihood.[1]

As explained in Chapter 7 above (page 72), under section 24(1) of the 1960 Act, local authorities have power to provide sites for gypsy caravans. In addition, section 24(2)(c) (added by section 80(2) of the 1994 Act) empowers local authorities to provide working space and facilities for the carrying on of activities normally carried on by gypsies. The former duty to provide and manage sites (in Part II of the 1968 Act) was repealed by section 80(1) of the 1994 Act.

Unauthorised Gypsy Sites

Section 77 of the 1994 Act empowers a local authority (in England, a county council, district council, London borough council, the Common Council of the City of London and the Council of the Isles of Scilly; in Wales, a county or county borough council) to direct persons

---

[1]   *R. v. South Hams District Council ex parte Gibb* [1994] 3 W.L.R. 1151.

residing unlawfully in vehicles within the authority's area on highway land, other unoccupied land or occupied land without the consent of the occupier, to leave the land and to remove their vehicles and any other property they have with them on the land. In exercising their power to make a direction, a local authority must make adequate enquiries as to the effect of eviction on the schooling of any child on the site, and on the health and welfare of any persons who may be vulnerable by reason of age, infirmity, sickness or pregnancy.[2] A person who fails to comply with a direction as soon as practicable commits an offence. It is also an offence for a person who has been directed to leave land to re-enter the land with a vehicle within three months of the date of the direction. The maximum penalty on conviction is a fine not exceeding Level 3 on the standard scale (currently £1,000). It is a defence to show that failure to comply with a direction, or returning to the land within three months, was due to mechanical breakdown, illness or other immediate emergency.

Section 78 of the 1994 Act provides that, on a complaint being made by a local authority, a magistrates' court may make an order requiring the removal from the land of any vehicle and property and any person residing in it and may authorise the authority to enter the land and remove the vehicle and property. It is an offence to obstruct anyone who has been authorised to carry out the order, for which the maximum penalty on conviction is a fine not exceeding Level 3 on the standard scale (currently £1,000).

General advice to local authorities on the provisions of the 1994 Act covering unauthorised camping is given in the Department of the Environment Circular 18/94 (Welsh Office Circular 76/94) entitled *Gypsy Sites Policy and Unauthorised Camping* dated 23rd November 1994 (ISBN 0-11-753022-0). Revised advice on the toleration of unauthorised gypsy sites is given in the Department of the

---

[2]   *R. v. Wolverhampton M.B.C. ex parte Dunne* [1997] 29 H.L.R. 745.

Environment, Transport and the Regions Circular entitled *Gypsy Sites Policy and Unauthorised Camping: ISBN 0-11-753022-0 Amendments to paragraphs 6-9 of DOE Circular 18/94, WO Circular 76/94. Revision of advice on "toleration",* dated 26th July 2000.

The wording of the revised advice issued in July 2000 is as follows:

6. Whilst it is a matter for local discretion to decide whether it is appropriate to evict an unauthorised Gypsy encampment, the Secretary of State believes that local authorities should consider using their powers to do so wherever the Gypsies concerned are causing a level of nuisance which cannot be effectively controlled. They also consider that it would usually be legitimate for a local authority to exercise these powers wherever Gypsies who are camped unlawfully refuse to move onto an authorised local authority site. Where there are no such sites, and the authority reaches the view that an unauthorised Gypsy encampment is not causing a level of nuisance which cannot be effectively controlled, it should consider providing basic services, such as toilets, a refuse skip and a supply of drinking water at that site.

7. Local authorities should also try to identify possible emergency stopping places, as close as possible to the transit routes used by Gypsies, where Gypsy families would be allowed to camp for short periods. Authorities should consider providing basic services on these temporary sites.

8. Where Gypsies are unlawfully camped on Government-owned land, it is for the local authority, with the agreement of the land-owning Department, to take any necessary steps to ensure that the encampment does not constitute a hazard to public health. It will continue to be the policy of

the Secretary of State that Government Departments should act in conformity with the advice that unauthorised encampments should not normally be allowed to continue where they are causing a level of nuisance which cannot be effectively controlled, particularly where local authority authorised sites are available. The National Assembly for Wales will act in the same way.

9. The Secretary of State continues to consider that local authorities should not use their powers to evict Gypsies needlessly. He considers that local authorities should use their powers in a humane and compassionate way, taking account of the rights and needs of the Gypsies concerned, the owners of the land in question, and the wider community whose lives may be affected by the situation.

Further advice on managing unauthorised camping is set out in *Managing Unauthorised Camping: A Good Practice Guide (Revision of Chapter 5)* issued by the Office of the Deputy Prime Minister in August 2000. (At the time of writing, the good practice guide itself is out of print.)

Gypsy Sites and Planning

Advice to local authorities on the planning aspects of gypsy sites is given in Department of the Environment Circular 1/94 (Welsh Office Circular 2/94). Although out of date in some respects (e.g. references to planning legislation), the circular remains in force.

Chapter 14

GYPSIES AND HUMAN RIGHTS LAW

Under the Human Rights Act 1998, the European Convention on Human Rights and Fundamental Freedoms has largely been incorporated into English law. There have been a number of cases where gypsies have claimed that their treatment by local authorities and others has been in breach of articles of the Convention.

A number of recent cases[1] have been brought before the European Court of Human Rights, alleging that the U.K. government was in breach of, among others, Articles 8 (right to respect for private and family life) and 14 (prohibition of discrimination). In all the cases the facts were similar. The applicants were all gypsies who had stationed caravans on land which they owned without obtaining planning permission. The local planning authorities successfully took enforcement action on the basis that the stationing of caravans was contrary to landscape or Green Belt policies or was impermissible on highway safety grounds. The gypsies argued that official gypsy sites were unsuitable or not available and that, consequently, they had nowhere else to go if they were not permitted to use their own land. In every case, the Court held that there had been no breach of the articles. The Court followed its own earlier decision in *Buckley v. U.K.* (1996) E. Com. H.R. 1271 that, on similar facts, there was no breach of either Article 8 or Article 14. In respect of Article 8, there was a proper regulatory framework for dealing with planning issues. In respect of Article 14, there was no discrimination against B as a gypsy; she was treated the same as others on planning matters.

---

[1]   *Varey v. U.K.* [2001] *The Times*, 30 January; *Chapman v. U.K., Coster v. U.K., Beard v. U.K., Lee v. U.K., Jane Smith v. U.K.* [2001] *The Times*, 30 January.

(It should be noted that the *Varey* case did not proceed to trial. It was withdrawn when the applicant received £60,000 in compensation and £15,000 costs from the U.K. government. The site in question had been used by gypsies for some time and had been granted a site licence by the local planning authority.)

These cases were followed by *Isaacs v. Secretary of State for Transport, Local Government and the Regions* [2002] E.W.H.C. 1014 (Admin.), in which I., a gypsy, who lived in a caravan on a site owned by a local authority, was given notice of termination of his licence. The authority began summary proceedings to recover possession in the county court. I. alleged that this amounted to a breach of his rights under Articles 8 (right of respect for private and family life) and 14 (prohibition of discrimination) of the Convention. The Administrative Court held that (i) the exemption of local authority owned sites from the protective provisions of the 1983 Act was necessary and justified in a democratic society and there was thus no breach of Article 8, and (ii) the exemption in section 5 of the 1983 Act depended upon the status of the site owner as a local authority and not on any personal quality of the licensee or tenant and there was thus no discrimination contrary to Article 14 of the Convention.

In the light of the foregoing cases, it is unlikely that measures to remove gypsies from unauthorised sites will be subject to challenge under the Human Rights Act 1998 save in exceptional circumstances.

Part IV

MISCELLANEOUS

Chapter 15

COUNCIL TAX AND NON-DOMESTIC RATING

Council Tax

Under the Local Government Finance Act 1992, a property tax, known as council tax, is payable in respect of dwellings. Liability to pay the tax accrues on a daily basis. Certain dwellings are exempt so long as they fall into one or more of the classes of exempt dwelling prescribed by the Secretary of State.[1] There are 23 classes of exemption, many of which depend on whether or not the dwelling is occupied as a residence. One such class relates specifically to caravans and boat moorings (see below).

The person liable to pay the council tax is, primarily, the person resident in the dwelling in question. If there are two or more residents, they are jointly and severally liable provided that they are the freehold owners of the dwelling or any part of it. In prescribed cases, where there is no person resident in the dwelling, the owner is liable (so long as the dwelling is not exempt). These cases mostly relate to residential care homes, nursing homes and the like, and dwellings occupied by religious communities.[2]

Where a person who is liable to pay the council tax is married to another person and both are resident in the dwelling, they are treated as spouses and are jointly and severally liable to pay the tax. For the purposes of the 1992 Act, two persons are married if they are a man and a woman who are either married to each other or are not married but are living together as husband and wife. It is

---

[1] Council Tax (Exempt Dwellings) Order 1992, S.I. 1992 No. 558 (as amended).

[2] Council Tax (Liability for Owners) Regulations 1992, S.I. 1992 No. 551 (as amended).

for consideration whether or not the decision in the *Mendoza* case (above, page 101) is applicable so as to treat same-sex partners as if they were living together as husband and wife.

The amount of council tax is set each year by the billing authority and is payable on a daily basis for each chargeable dwelling. All chargeable dwellings are placed in one of eight valuation bands as follows:

	England	*Wales*
A:	£1-40,000	£1-30,000
B:	£40,001-52,000	£30,001-39,000
C:	£52,001-68,000	£39,001-51,000
D:	£68,001-88,000	£51,001-66,000
E:	£88,001-120,000	£66,001-90,000
F:	£120,001-160,000	£90,001-120,000
G:	£160,001-320,000	£120,001-240,000
H:	Exceeding £320,000	Exceeding £240,000

The value of a dwelling is as at 1st April 1991. The 1992 Act enables revaluations to take place but none has so far been undertaken.

The basic amount of council tax payable is the same for all dwellings in a valuation band in the area of each billing authority. The amount is set by the billing authority in the light of its budget requirement, calculated in accordance with the provisions of the 1992 Act. However, there are certain discounts available, as follows:

(1) Where there is only one resident in a dwelling, a discount of 25% applies.

(2) Where there is no resident of the dwelling, a discount of 50% applies.

(3) Where there are two or more residents of the dwelling and each of them is disregarded for the purposes of

discount, the 50% discount applies. Disregarded persons include prisoners, the severely mentally impaired, students and apprentices, hospital patients, residents in care homes, nursing homes and the like, certain care workers and residents in shelters and similar accommodation.

There are detailed provisions in both the 1992 Act and in regulations made under the Act covering payment, administration and enforcement of the council tax. These are principally the responsibility of the billing authorities: in England, district councils, unitary councils, London borough councils and the Council of the Isles of Scilly; in Wales, county and county borough councils.

There are some special provisions relating to caravans and caravan sites, as follows:

(1) A caravan which is a person's only or main residence is subject to council tax as a dwelling and the resident is the person liable to pay the tax.[3] The amount of the tax depends upon the valuation band in which the dwelling falls and the level of tax charged by the billing authority in respect of that band.[4]

(2) Where on any day the owner of a caravan is not resident in it, but someone else is, that other person is liable to pay the council tax. Where there is no such other person (i.e. the caravan is unoccupied), the owner is liable to pay.[5]

(3) A dwelling which consists of a pitch or mooring which is not occupied by a caravan or, as the case may be, a boat falls within Class R in the classes of exempt dwellings and council tax is not therefore payable in respect of it.

---

[3] Local Government Finance Act 1992, ss. 3 and 6.
[4] Local Government Finance Act 1992, s. 5.
[5] Local Government Finance Act 1992, s. 7.

Non-Domestic Rates

Premises which are not occupied for residential purposes are, as a general rule, subject to the payment of non-domestic rates.[6] To be liable for non-domestic rates, premises must normally be exclusively occupied by a person, or by persons jointly, for his or their own benefit for a period which is not merely transient. Thus, for example, a person who occupies a site for a short period for a travelling show is not in rateable occupation of the site.

To be liable for non-domestic rates, premises must be shown in the local valuation list.[7] There are classes of property which are exempt from non-domestic rating and others where some form of relief from the payment of all or some of the amount of rates is available. The main exemptions from rating are:

(1) Agricultural land and buildings (including fish farms).

(2) Places of religious worship.

(3) Parks provided by local authorities and available for free and unrestricted use by members of the public.

(4) Property used by the disabled.

(5) Property in enterprise zones.

(6) Property occupied by visiting forces.

Relief from some or all non-domestic rates is available to charities and to certain general stores, food stores and post offices in rural settlements where the population does not exceed 3,000.

The amount of non-domestic rates payable in respect of a rateable property is calculated by multiplying the rateable value by the non-domestic rating multiplier and dividing

---

[6]   Local Government Finance Act 1988, s. 42.
[7]   Local Government Finance Act 1988, s. 42

the resulting sum by the number of days in the financial year. The multiplier is an amount in pence per pound and is set annually by the Secretary of State. Where a property is unoccupied for more than three months, 50% of the full amount of rates is payable, with exemptions for industrial buildings, listed buildings and small properties with rateable values of less than £1,900.

The rateable value of a rateable property broadly represents the yearly rent at which the property could have been let on the open market on 1st April 1998. There are special provisions in the 1988 Act[8] relating to the alteration of the rateable value of a caravan site which permit the nature of the caravan on the pitch and the physical condition of the caravan to be taken into account as factors affecting the rateable value.

A pitch occupied by a caravan is a non-domestic property, unless the caravan is the sole or main residence of an individual, in which case the pitch and the caravan, together with any garden, yard, outhouse or other appurtenance enjoyed with or belonging to them are domestic property (and thus subject to council tax).[9]

Certain caravan sites with permanently sited caravans on them which are the sole or main residence of no-one are normally subject to non-domestic rates. The circumstances in which this situation applies are specified in the Non-Domestic Rating (Caravan Sites) Regulations 1990 (S.I. 1990 No. 673), as amended by the Non-Domestic Rating (Caravan Sites) (Amendment) Regulations 1991 (S.I. 1991 No. 471). The Regulations provide that, where pitches for caravans on a "relevant site" (i.e. a site where (a) some property is non-domestic, and (b) the site area is 400 square yards or more) would constitute separate hereditaments because they are occupied by persons other than the site operator, those pitches are to be treated

---

[8]   Local Government Finance Act 1988, Sch. 6, para. 2B.
[9]   Local Government Finance Act 1988, s. 66(3).

as one hereditament in the occupation of the site operator. This is most likely to be the case where the caravans are holiday caravans. A site operator must be given written details of the caravan pitches subject to the 1990 and 1991 Regulations shown on the valuation list. Any person occupying a pitch on a relevant site may, on giving reasonable notice to the valuation officer, inspect a copy of the information supplied to the site operator.

Chapter 16

ROAD TRAFFIC CONTROL

This chapter is concerned with road traffic law as it applies to the ordinary holiday caravan on the road. Mobile homes in transit will also fall under the general provisions.

The essential law is contained in the Road Traffic Act 1988 and in regulations made pursuant to the Act. For convenience, the Act and regulations will be treated separately. There are so many detailed and technical regulations that only the most important ones are considered here.

The Road Traffic Act in Relation to Caravans

The word "caravan" does not appear in the 1988 Act at all. There can be no doubt, however, that it falls within the definition of "trailer" contained in section 185(1). For the purpose of the Act, a motor vehicle is expressed to mean a mechanically propelled vehicle intended or adapted for use on roads. A trailer is defined as a vehicle drawn by a motor vehicle.

Apart from the general definition, the Secretary of State is empowered, under the Act, to make regulations relating to, *inter alia*, the construction and use of trailers, their equipment and the conditions under which they may be used on roads.[1]

The Motor Vehicles (Construction and Use) Regulations 1986 (S.I. 1986 No. 1078) (as amended) have been made pursuant to the Act and, insofar as they have application to caravans, deal with such matters as brakes and tyres, maximum dimensions for road use, trailer plates, etc. In addition to the above Regulations, the Road Vehicles

---

[1]   Road Traffic Act 1988, s. 41.

Lighting Regulations 1989 (S. I. 1989 No. 1796) (as amended) have effect. These provisions are relevant to caravans on the road.

It is an offence to contravene construction and use requirements as follows:

(i) relating to brakes, steering gear and tyres (s. 41A of the 1988 Act);

(ii) relating to the weight of certain goods and passenger vehicles (s. 41B of the 1988 Act); and

(iii) relating to other such requirements (s. 42 of the 1988 Act).

The offences are fixed penalty offences within Schedule 3 to the Road Traffic Offenders Act 1988. The amount of the fixed penalty is prescribed in the Fixed Penalty Order 2000 (S.I. 2000 No. 2792) and is £60 where the offence carries with it an obligatory licence endorsement and normally £30 in other cases. (An explanation of the fixed penalty system is outside the scope of this book.)

In addition to offences against construction and use regulations, section 60 of the Road Traffic Act 1988 creates two other general offences in relation to trailers which may be applied to caravans. These are of importance so far as dealers in caravans are concerned.

Section 75(1) of the 1988 Act makes it an offence to sell or supply (or to offer to do so) a trailer for delivery in such a condition that its use on the road in that condition would be unlawful in respect of any provisions as to brakes, steering gear or tyres or as to construction, weight or equipment. It is also an offence to sell, etc. a trailer in such a condition that its use on the road would involve a danger of injury to any person.

Section 75(4) of the 1988 Act creates an offence of so altering a trailer as to render its condition such that its use on a road in that condition would be unlawful.

It is a defence in respect of each of the above offences for a person charged to prove:

(i) that the trailer was sold, supplied, offered or altered for export from Great Britain; or

(ii) that he had reasonable cause to believe that the trailer would not be used on a road in Great Britain, or would not be used until it could, by its condition, have been used lawfully.[2]

There is one other part of the 1988 Act that calls for consideration in the context of caravans. By virtue of section 34 thereof, it is an offence for a person, without lawful authority, to drive a motor vehicle on to or upon any common land, moorland or other land not forming part of a road, or on any footpath or bridleway. It is not, however, an offence to do so within fifteen yards of a road on which a motor vehicle may lawfully be driven provided that it is merely for the purpose of parking.[3]

The section has an obvious relevance to caravans because a trailer cannot (by definition) be drawn except by a motor vehicle. It will be recalled that there are many statutory provisions prohibiting the use of caravans on commons.[4] In practice, section 34 is another such prohibition.

Constuction and Use Regulations

The most important of the Motor Vehicles (Construction and Use) Regulations 1986 (as amended) may be summarised as set out below.

(1) Brakes
Every caravan, manufactured on or after 1st October 1982 and exceeding 750 kilograms in weight must be equipped with an efficient braking system.

---

[2] Road Traffic Act 1988, s. 75(6).
[3] Road Traffic Act 1988, s. 34(3).
[4] See ch. 7.

If the brakes do not come into operation automatically on the overrun of the caravan, the braking system must be so designed and constructed that:

(1) When the caravan is being drawn, the operation of its braking system is activated by the application of the main brake of the towing vehicle. In the event of a failure there must be a secondary means of operation.

(2) When the caravan is stationary, a handbrake is required which is capable of being applied to at least two wheels of the caravan. It must be maintained in operation by direct mechanical action without the intervention of any hydraulic, electric or pneumatic device. It must also be capable of holding the caravan stationary on a gradient of at least 1 in 6.25 without the assistance of stored energy.

(2) Towing of Caravans
There are several regulations governing the way in which caravans should be towed on the road, including restrictions on the distance between the caravan and the towing vehicle.

Certain vehicles are automatically excluded from towing, namely:

(i)   a motor cycle not exceeding 125cc;

(ii) any motor cycle where the towed vehicle exceeds 254 kilograms in weight or 1 metre in width;

(iii) an invalid carriage or straddle carrier;

(iv) a bus.

In addition, passengers may not be carried in a caravan whilst it is moving on the road. The only exception to this is that passengers are permitted where a caravan is being tested by its manufacturer, or by a repairer, distributor or dealer.

The provisions relating to the distance between caravan and trailer are as follows:

(1) The maximum permitted length of a combination of vehicles (i.e. trailer and towing vehicle) is 18.75 metres. In the case of a breakdown, this figure may be exceeded.

(2) Where a motor vehicle is drawing a caravan solely by means of a rope or chain, the length of the rope or chain is required to be such that the distance between the nearest points of the caravan and towing vehicle cannot exceed 4.5 metres.

(3) Where a motor vehicle is drawing a caravan and the distance between the nearest points of the respective vehicles exceeds 1.5 metres, steps must be taken to render the means by which the caravan is attached clearly visible to other road users.

(3) Overall Length and Width
Subject to certain exceptions (which are not relevant in this context), the overall length of a caravan must not exceed 7 metres. For the purpose of the regulation, the term "overall length" specifically excludes any part of the caravan designed primarily for use as a means of attaching it to another vehicle (e.g. a drawbar) and any fitting designed for use with that part.

The overall width of a caravan should not exceed 2.3 metres.

(4) Tyres
Every caravan, when drawn on the road, must have every wheel fitted with a pneumatic tyre. There are various safety requirements, all of which are important. In particular, re-cut tyres must not be used or tyres which have a break in the fabric or any portion of the ply or cord structure exposed.

(5) Weight
The essential provisions as to weight are:

(i)   the total laden weight transmitted to the road surface by any two wheels of a caravan in line transversely must not exceed 10,500 kilograms;

(ii) the total laden weight of the caravan must not, in any event, exceed 14,230 kilograms.

Lighting Regulations
Certain of the Road Vehicles Lighting Regulations 1989[5] are important so far as caravans are concerned.

(1) Direction Indicators
Caravans are generally required to have amber flashing indicators at the rear.

Where direction indicators are required, they must flash in unison with those of the towing vehicle at a speed of between 60-120 flashes per minute. The system must have provision for the driver to be made aware of the failure of any one of the indicators on the caravan or towcar.

Direction indicators, when fitted, must be maintained in a clean condition and in good and efficient working order.

(2) Lights
Every caravan must have two rear lamps which conform to certain size requirements or, in the case of modern caravans, bear a particular approval mark.

Both lamps must have the same appearance, when illuminated, and the same illuminated area. If such lamps are electrically operated, the wiring must be so arranged as to prevent both lamps being extinguished in the event of one of the bulbs failing. Bulbs must be at least 5 watts, and the rated wattage should be marked on the bulb.

---

[5]   S.I. 1989 No. 1796 (as amended).

If the lamps are circular, the area illuminated must be at least 2 inches in diameter. If not circular, the area illuminated must not be less than the area of a circle of 2 inches in diameter and of such a shape that a circle of 1 inch diameter may be inscribed therein. No part of the illuminated area may be more than 3 feet 6 inches from the ground or less than 15 inches.

No part of a caravan may extend laterally more than 16 inches beyond the illuminated area of the lamp. Forward facing sidelights, visible to oncoming traffic, are required if the caravan extends laterally more than 12 inches beyond the centre of the sidelights of the towing car.

(3) Reflectors
Two triangular reflectors are required on all caravans at the rear. They must not be more than 3 feet 6 inches from the ground to the highest point of the reflector, and not less than 15 inches from the ground to the lowest point. Reflectors must be not less than 21 inches apart and at the same height from the ground as each other.

Where a caravan exceeds 5 metres in length, it is required to have two amber reflectors on each side if it is used on the road during the hours of darkness.

(4) Stop Lights
Every caravan manufactured before 1st January 1971 is required to be fitted with a stop light. This must be fitted at the rear of the vehicle and on the offside. A second stop light may be fitted on the nearside.

In the case of caravans manufactured after 1st January 1971, two stop lights must be fitted. They must be symmetric-ally positioned and be at the same height from the ground.

Miscellaneous
Three important matters are not covered by any of the above regulations but will be of concern to the family motorist.

(1) Licence Requirements

It is not necessary to have a special driving licence in order to tow a caravan. However, holders of provisional driving licences may not drive a vehicle towing a caravan except when they have passed a test authorising them to be granted a full licence.[6]

(2) Insurance

Section 143 of the Road Traffic Act 1988 requires all users of motor vehicles to be insured or secured against third party risks. Use of a motor vehicle when drawing a trailer (including a caravan) is an offence if the policy does not expressly cover such use.[7]

Although most insurance policies will cover towing, they are unlikely to cover damage caused to or by the caravan when it is not being towed and is, for example, standing in the owner's drive. There is no legal requirement to obtain such cover but the prudent caravan owner will no doubt do so.

(3) Speed Limits

In general there is a maximum speed limit of 50 miles per hour on all roads in respect of caravans that are being towed, provided that there is not a lower speed limit in force. The limit is raised to 60 miles per hour on dual carriageways and motorways.

It should be observed that it is an offence for a motor vehicle towing a caravan to use the outside lane of a three-lane carriageway. No offence is committed, however, in so far as it is necessary for such vehicle to be driven to enable it to pass another vehicle which is carrying or drawing a load of exceptional width.[8]

---

6 See the Motor Vehicles (Driving Licences) Regulations 1999, S.I. 1999 No. 2864 (as amended).
7 *Robb v. M'Kechnie* [1936] S.C.(J.) 25.
8 The Motorways Traffic (England and Wales) Regulations 1982, S.I. 1982 No. 1163, reg. 12.

Chapter 17

TAXATION

Value Added Tax

All suppliers of goods and services must pay value added tax, where their annual turnover exceeds £55,000, except where the goods or services are exempt or zero rated.[1]

Caravans exceeding the size permitted for lawful use on the roads as trailers are zero rated. Caravans below these limits are taxed at a positive rate. At present the rate is 17.5 per cent.[2]

Case Law

(1) Capital Gains Tax

In *Makins v. Elson (Inspector of Taxes)*,[3] a taxpayer owned a site on which he lived with his family in a caravan. When he sold the land, he was assessed to capital gains tax. He appealed on the basis that the caravan came within the definition of a "dwelling house" and that it was his only or main residence. Foster J. held, in the Chancery Division, that the appeal should be allowed. The caravan had water, electricity and a telephone, and it came within the definition of a dwelling house for taxation purposes.

By contrast, in *Moore v. Thompson (Inspector of Taxes)*,[4] it was held that a wheeled caravan with no mains services was not a dwelling house and its disposal was subject to the payment of capital gains tax.

(2) Capital Allowances

In *Cooke (Inspector of Taxes) v. Beach Station Caravans Ltd.*,[5]

---

[1] The Value Added Tax Act 1994, s. 3, Sch. I (as amended).
[2] This rate is subject to fluctuation.
[3] [1977] 1 All E.R. 572.
[4] [1986] S.T.C. 170.
[5] [1974] 3 All E.R. 159.

the taxpayer company owned and operated a caravan site. They constructed a swimming pool and paddling pool on site. The Crown accepted that a certain portion of the expenditure was eligible for tax relief as being "machinery or plant" within the meaning or sections 18(1) and 19(1) of the Capital Allowances Act 1968 (now section 24 of the Capital Allowances Act 1990). It was argued, however, that expenditure on pool construction, excavation and terracing did not attract relief.

Megarry J. held, in the Chancery Division, that all the expenditure was eligible for relief. When considered in relation to the company's business, the pools were not for an ornamental purpose but were designed to attract custom to the site. The pools were, accordingly, "plant" provided by the company for the purposes of its trade.

APPENDICES

Appendix A

MODEL STANDARDS FOR PERMANENT RESIDENTIAL MOBILE HOME SITES

issued by the Secretaries of State for the Environment and for Wales under the Caravan Sites and Control of Development Act 1960 (Revised 1989)

I. Section 5(6) of the Act provides that the Secretary of State may from time to time specify Model Standards with respect to the lay-out and the provision of facilities, services and equipment for caravan sites or particular types of caravan site; and that, in deciding what (if any) conditions to attach to a site licence, the local authority shall have regard to any standards so specified.

Section 7(1) provides that on an appeal against any condition of a site licence a magistrates' court, if satisfied, having regard amongst other things to any standards specified by the Secretary of State under section 5(6), that a condition is unduly burdensome, may vary or cancel the condition.

Section 24, which empowers local authorities to provide caravan sites, provides in subsection (2) that in exercising their powers under the section the local authority shall have regard to any standards that may have been specified by the Secretary of State under section 5(6) of the Act.

II. In pursuance of his powers under section 5(6) of the Act, the Secretary of State hereby specifies the following standards in relation to caravan sites on which some or all of the caravans are used as permanent residences by people other than gypsies or agricultural workers. They are Model Standards: they represent the standards normally to be expected as a matter of good practice on such sites. They are not intended to apply to any other type of caravan site – for example, sites which only have holiday caravans, or touring caravan sites. They should be applied with due regard to the particular circumstances of each case, including the physical character of the site, any services or facilities that may already be available within convenient reach, and other local conditions.

Site Boundaries

1. The boundaries of the site should be clearly marked, for example by fences or hedges. In addition, the site owner should give the local authority a plan of its layout. It is recommended that a 3-metre wide area should be kept clear within the inside of all boundaries.

Density and Space Between Caravans

2. Subject to the following variations, every caravan should be not less than 6 metres from any other caravan which is occupied separately and not less than 2 metres from a road. The point of measurement for porches, awnings etc. is the exterior cladding of the caravan.

- Porches may protrude 1 metre into the 6 metres and should be of the open type.

- Where awnings are used, the distance between any part of the awning and an adjoining caravan should not be less than 3 metres. They should not be of the type which incorporates sleeping accommodation and they should not face each other or touch.

- Eaves, drainpipes and bay windows may extend into the 6 metre space provided the total distance between the extremities of two adjacent units is not less than 5.25 metres.

- Where there are ramps for the disabled, verandahs and stairs extending from the unit, there should be 4.5

metres clear space between them and two such items should not face each other in any space. If they are enclosed, they may need to be considered as part of the unit and, as such, should not intrude into the 6 metre space.

‐ A garage, a shed or a covered storage space should be permitted between units only if it is of non-combustible construction (including non-combustible roof) and sufficient space is maintained around each unit so as not to prejudice means of escape in case of fire. Windows in such structures should not face towards the units on either side. Car ports and covered walkways should in no circumstances be allowed within the 6-metre space. For cars and boats between units, see Standard 27.

3. The density should be consistent with safety standards and health and safety requirements. The gross density should not exceed 50 caravans to the hectare, calculated on the basis of the useable area (i.e. excluding lakes, roads, communal services and other areas unsuitable for the siting of caravans) rather than the total site area.

Roads, Gateways and Footpaths
4. Roads and footpaths should be designed to provide adequate access for fire appliances. (Detailed guidance on turning circles etc. is available from fire authorities.) Roads of suitable material should be provided so that no caravan standing is more than 50 metres from a road. Where the approach to the caravan is across ground that may become difficult or dangerous to negotiate in wet weather, each standing should be connected to a carriageway by a footpath with a hard surface. Roads should not be less than 3.7 metres wide, or, if they form part of a clearly-marked one way traffic system, 3 metres wide. Gateways should be a minimum of 3.1 metres wide and have a minimum height clearance of 3.7 metres. Footpaths should not be less than 0.75 metres wide. Roads

should have no overhead cable less than 4.5 metres above the ground. Roads and footpaths should be suitably lit. Emergency vehicle routes within the site should be kept clear of obstruction at all times.

Hard Standings

5. Every caravan should stand on a concrete hard-standing which should extend over the whole area occupied by the caravan placed upon it, and should project a sufficient distance outwards from its entrance or entrances to enable occupants to enter and leave safely.

Fire Fighting Appliances

Fire Points

6. These should be established so that no caravan or site building is more than 30 metres from a fire point. They should be housed in a weather-proof structure, easily accessible and clearly and conspicuously marked "FIRE POINT".

Fire Fighting Equipment

7. Where water standpipes are provided and there is a water supply of sufficient pressure and flow to project a jet of water approximately 5 metres from the nozzle, such water standpipes should be situated at each fire point. There should also be a reel that complies with British Standard 5306 Part 1, with a hose not less than 30 metres long, having a means of connection to a water standpipe (preferably a screw thread connection) with a water supply of sufficient pressure and terminating in a small hand control nozzle. Hoses should be housed in a box painted red and marked "HOSE REEL".

8. Where standpipes are not provided but there is a water supply of sufficient pressure and flow, fire hydrants should be installed within 100 metres of every caravan standing. Hydrants should conform to British Standard 750. Access to hydrants and other water supplies should not be obstructed or obscured.

9. Where standpipes are not provided or the water pressure or flow is not sufficient, each fire point should be provided with either water extinguishers (2 x 9 litre) or a water tank of at least 500 litres capacity fitted with a hinged cover, 2 buckets and 1 hand pump or bucket pump.

Fire Warning

10. A means of raising the alarm in the event of a fire should be provided at each fire point. This could be by means of a manually operated sounder, e.g. metal triangle with a striker, gong or hand operated siren. The advice of the fire authority should be sought on an appropriate system.

Maintenance

11. All alarm and fire fighting equipment should be installed, tested and maintained in working order by a competent person and be available for inspection by, or on behalf of, the licensing authority. A log book should be kept to record all tests and any remedial action.

12. All equipment susceptible to damage by frost should be suitably protected.

Fire Notices

13. A clearly written and conspicuous notice should be provided and maintained at each fire point to indicate the action to be taken in case of fire and the location of the nearest telephone. This notice should include the following:

"On discovering a fire:

i.   ensure the caravan or site building involved is evacuated;

ii. raise the alarm;

iii. call the fire brigade (the nearest telephone is sited ....);

iv. attack the fire using the fire fighting equipment provided, if safe to do so.

It is in the interest of all occupiers of this site to be familiar with the above routine and the method of operating the fire alarm and fire fighting equipment."

Fire Hazards

14. Long grass and vegetation should be cut at frequent and regular intervals where necessary to prevent it becoming a fire hazard to caravans, buildings or other installations on the site. Any such cuttings should be removed from the vicinity of caravans. The space beneath and between caravans should not be used for the storage of combustible materials.

Telephones

15. An immediately accessible telephone should be available on the site for calling the emergency services. A notice by the telephone should include the address of the site.

Storage of Liquefied Petroleum Gas (LPG)

16. LPG supplied from tanks should comply with Guidance Booklet HSG 34 "The Storage of LPG at Fixed Installations" or, where LPG is supplied from cylinders, with Guidance Note CS4 "The Keeping of LPG in Cylinders and Similar Containers" as appropriate.

Where there are metered supplies from a common LPG storage tank, then Guidance Note CS11 "The Storage and Use of LPG at Metered Estates" provides further guidance. In this case and where a British Gas mains supply is available, then the Gas Safety (Installation and Use) Regulations 1984 and the Pipe-lines Act 1962 may also be applicable.

Exposed gas bottles or cylinders should not be within the separation boundary of an adjoining unit.

LPG installations should conform to British Standard 5482, "Code of Practice for domestic butane and propane gas burning installations, Part 2: 1977 Installations in Caravans and non-permanent dwellings".

For mains gas supply, the 1984 Regulations will be relevant for the installation downstream of any service pipe(s) supplying any primary meter(s) and such service pipes are subject to the Gas Safety Regulations 1972.

In cases where the site owner supplies gas to caravans on the site, he may need an authorisation to do so from OFGAS under the Gas Act 1986.

Electrical Installations

17. Sites should be provided with an electricity supply sufficient in all respects to meet all reasonable demands of the caravans situated on them.

18. Any electrical installations, which are not Electricity Board works and circuits subject to regulations made by the Secretary of State under section 16 of the Energy Act 1983 and section 64 of the Electricity Act 1947, should be installed, tested and maintained in accordance with the provisions of the Institution of Electrical Engineers' (IEE) Regulations for Electrical Installations for the time being in force, and where appropriate, to the standard which would be acceptable for the purposes of the Electricity Supply Regulations 1988, Statutory Instrument 1988 No. 1057.

19. Work on electrical installations and appliances should be carried out only by competent persons such as the manufacturer's appointed agent, the electricity supplier, a professionally qualified electrical engineer, a member of the Electrical Contractors' Association, a contractor approved by the National Inspection Council for Electrical Installation Contracting, or a qualified person acting on behalf of one of the above. The installations should be inspected periodically: under IEE Wiring Regulations, every year or such longer period (not exceeding 3 years) as is considered appropriate in each case. When an installation is inspected, it should be judged against the current regulations.

The inspector should, within 1 month of such an inspection, issue an inspection certificate in the form prescribed in the IEE Wiring Regulations which should be retained by the site operator and displayed, supplemented or replaced by subsequent certificates, with the site licence. The cost of the inspection and report should be met by the site operator or licence holder.

20. If an inspection reveals that an installation no longer complies with the regulations extant at the time it was first installed, any deficiencies should be rectified. Any major alterations and extensions to an installation and all parts of the existing installation affected by them should comply with the latest version of the IEE Wiring Regulations.

21. If there are overhead electric lines on the site, suitable warning notices should be displayed at the entrance to the site and on supports for the line. Where appropriate, particular attention should be drawn to the danger of masts of yachts or dinghies contacting the line.

Water Supply
22. All parks should be provided with a water supply in accordance with appropriate Water Byelaws and statutory quality standards.

Drainage, Sanitation and Washing Facilities
23. Satisfactory provision should be made for foul drainage, either by connection to a public sewer or sewage treatment works or by discharge to a properly constructed septic tank or cesspool approved by the local authority.

24. Each caravan should have its own water supply and water closet. Each caravan standing should be provided with a connection to the foul drainage system; the connection should be capable of being made air-tight when not in use.

25. Every site and every hard standing should be provided with an adequate drainage system for the complete and

hygienic disposal of foul, rain and surface water from the site, buildings, caravans, roads and footpaths.

Refuse Disposal

26. Every caravan standing should have an adequate number of suitable non-combustible refuse bins with close-fitting lids or plastic bags. Arrangements should be made for the bins to be emptied regularly. Where communal refuse bins are also provided these should be of similar construction and housed within a properly constructed bin store.

Parking

27. One car only may be parked between adjoining caravans provided that the door to the caravan is not obstructed. Suitably surfaced parking spaces should be provided where necessary to meet the additional requirements of the occupants and their visitors. Plastic or wooden boats should not be parked between units.

Recreation Space

28. Where children live on the site, space equivalent to about one-tenth of the total area should be allocated for children's games and/or other recreational purposes. This provision will normally be necessary because of the limited space available round the caravans, but may be omitted where there are suitable alternative publicly provided recreational facilities which are readily accessible.

Notices

29. A suitable sign should be prominently displayed at the site entrance indicating the name of the site.

30. A copy of the site licence with its conditions should be displayed prominently on the site.

31. Notices and a plan should be displayed on the site setting out the action to be taken in the event of an

emergency. They should show where the police, fire brigade, ambulance, and local doctors can be contacted, and the location of the nearest public telephone. The notices should also give the name and location/telephone number of the site licence holder or his/her accredited representative. At sites subject to flood risk, warning notices should be displayed giving advice about the operation of the flood warning system.

32. All notices should be suitably protected from the weather and displayed where possible out of the direct rays of the sun, preferably in areas lit by artificial lighting.

MODEL STANDARDS FOR HOLIDAY CARAVAN SITES

issued by the Secretaries of State for the Environment and for Wales under the Caravan Sites and Control of Development Act 1960, section 5 (Revised 1989)

I. Section 5(6) of the Act provides that the Secretary of State may from time to time specify Model Standards with respect to the lay-out and the provision of facilities, services and equipment for caravan sites or particular types of caravan site; and that, in deciding what (if any) conditions to attach to a site licence, the local authority shall have regard to any standards so specified.

Section 7(1) provides that on an appeal against any condition of a site licence a magistrates' court, if satisfied, having regard amongst other things to any standards specified by the Secretary of State under section 5(6), that a condition is unduly burdensome, may vary or cancel the condition.

Section 24, which empowers local authorities to provide caravan sites, provides in subsection (2) that in exercising their powers under the section the local authority shall have regard to any standards that may have been specified by the Secretary of State under section 5(6) of the Act.

II. In pursuance of his powers under section 5(6) of the Act, the Secretary of State hereby specifies the following standards in relation to holiday caravan sites. They are Model Standards: they represent the standards normally to be expected as a matter of good practice, on such sites.

They are not intended to apply to any other type of caravan site – for example, sites which only have caravans for permanent residential use, touring caravan sites, gypsy sites or sites which are used by agricultural workers. They should be applied with due regard to the particular circumstances of each case, including the physical character of the site, any services or facilities that may already be available within convenient reach, and other local conditions.

Site Boundaries

1. The boundaries of the site should be clearly marked, for example by fences or hedges. In addition, the site owner should give the local authority a plan of its layout. It is recommended that a 3-metre wide area should be kept clear within the inside of all boundaries.

Density and Space Between Caravans

2. Subject to the following variations, the minimum spacing distance between caravans made of aluminium or other materials with similar fire performance properties should be not less than 5 metres between units, 3.5 metres at the corners. (See specimen layout at Appendix 1.) For those with a plywood or similar skin it should be not less than 6 metres. Where there is a mixture of holiday caravans of aluminium and plywood, the separation distance should be 6 metres; and where there is a mixture of permanent residential homes and holiday caravans, the separation distance should again be 6 metres. The point of measurement for porches, awnings etc. is the exterior cladding of the caravan.

-   Porches may protrude 1 metre into the 5 metres and should be of the open type.

-   Where awnings are used, the distance between any part of the awning and an adjoining caravan should not be less than 3 metres. They should not be of the type which incorporates sleeping accommodation and they should not face each other or touch.

– Eaves, drainpipes and bay windows may extend into the 5 metre space provided the total distance between the extremities of two adjacent units is not less than 4.5 metres.

– Where there are ramps for the disabled, verandahs and stairs extending from the unit, there should be 3.5 metres clear space between them (4.5 metres if mixture of caravans) and such items should not face each other in any space. If they are enclosed, they may need to be considered as part of the unit and, as such, should not intrude into the 5 metre (or 6 metre) space.

– A garage, a shed or a covered storage space should be permitted between units only if it is of non-combustible construction (including non-combustible roof) and sufficient space is maintained around each unit so as not to prejudice means of escape in case of fire. Windows in such structures should not face towards the units on either side. Car ports and covered walkways should in no circumstances be allowed within the 5 or 6-metre space. For cars and boats between units, see Standard 27.

3. The density should be consistent with safety standards and health and amenity requirements. The gross density should not exceed 60 caravans to the hectare, calculated on the basis of the useable area (i.e. excluding lakes, roads, communal services and other areas unsuitable for the siting of caravans) rather than the total site area.

Roads, Gateways and Footpaths

4. Roads and footpaths should be designed to provide adequate access for fire appliances. (Detailed guidance on turning circles etc. is available from fire authorities.) Roads of suitable material should be provided so that no caravan standing is more than 50 metres from a road. Where the approach to the caravan is across ground that may become difficult or dangerous to negotiate in wet

weather, each standing should be connected to a carriageway by a footpath with a hard surface. Roads should not be less than 3.7 metres wide, or, if they form part of a clearly-marked one way traffic system, 3 metres wide. Gateways should be a minimum of 3.1 metres wide and have a minimum height clearance of 3.7 metres. Footpaths should not be less than 0.75 metres wide. Roads should have no overhead cable less than 4.5 metres above the ground. They should be suitably lit taking into account the needs and characteristics of a particular site. Emergency vehicle routes within the site should be kept clear of obstruction at all times.

Hard Standings
5. Where possible, every caravan should stand on a hard-standing of suitable material, which should extend over the whole area occupied by the caravan placed upon it, and should project a sufficient distance outwards from the entrance or entrances of the caravan to enable occupants to enter and leave safely.

Hard standings may be dispensed with if the caravans are removed during the winter, or if they are situated on ground which is firm and safe in poor weather conditions.

Fire Fighting Appliances
Fire Points
6. These should be established so that no caravan or site building is more than 30 metres from a fire point. They should be housed in a weather-proof structure, easily accessible and clearly and conspicuously marked "FIRE POINT".

Fire Fighting Equipment
7. Where water standpipes are provided and there is a water supply of sufficient pressure and flow to project a jet of water approximately 5 metres from the nozzle, such water standpipes should be situated at each fire point.

There should also be a reel that complies with British Standard 5306 Part 1, with a hose not less than 30 metres long, having a means of connection to a water standpipe (preferably a screw thread connection) with a water supply of sufficient pressure and terminating in a small hand control nozzle. Hoses should be housed in a box painted red and marked "HOSE REEL".

8. Where standpipes are not provided but there is a water supply of sufficient pressure and flow, fire hydrants should be installed within 100 metres of every caravan standing. Hydrants should conform to British Standard 750. Access to hydrants and other water supplies should not be obstructed or obscured.

9. Where standpipes are not provided or the water pressure or flow is not sufficient, each fire point should be provided with either water extinguishers (2 x 9 litre) or a water tank of at least 500 litres capacity fitted with a hinged cover, 2 buckets and 1 hand pump or bucket pump.

Fire Warning

10. A means of raising the alarm in the event of a fire should be provided at each fire point. This could be by means of a manually operated sounder, e.g. metal triangle with a striker, gong or hand operated siren. The advice of the fire authority should be sought on an appropriate system.

Maintenance

11. All alarm and fire fighting equipment should be installed, tested and maintained in working order by a competent person and be available for inspection by, or on behalf of, the licensing authority. A log book should be kept to record all tests and any remedial action.

12. All equipment susceptible to damage by frost should be suitably protected.

Fire Notices

13. A clearly written and conspicuous notice should be provided and maintained at each fire point to indicate the action to be taken in case of fire and the location of the nearest telephone. This notice should include the following:

"On discovering a fire:

i.   ensure the caravan or site building involved is evacuated;

ii. raise the alarm;

iii. call the fire brigade (the nearest telephone is sited ....);

iv. attack the fire using the fire fighting equipment provided, if safe to do so.

It is in the interest of all occupiers of this site to be familiar with the above routine and the method of operating the fire alarm and fire fighting equipment."

Fire Hazards

14. Long grass and vegetation should be cut at frequent and regular intervals where necessary to prevent it becoming a fire hazard to caravans, buildings or other installations on the site. Any such cuttings should be removed from the vicinity of caravans. The space beneath and between caravans should not be used for the storage of combustible materials.

Telephones

15. An immediately accessible telephone should be available on the site for calling the emergency services. A notice by the telephone should include the address of the site.

Storage of Liquefied Petroleum Gas (LPG)

16. LPG supplied from tanks should comply with Guidance Booklet HSG 34 "The Storage of LPG at Fixed Installations"

or, where LPG is supplied from cylinders, with Guidance Note CS4 "The Keeping of LPG in Cylinders and Similar Containers" as appropriate.

Where there are metered supplies from a common LPG storage tank, then Guidance Note CS11 "The Storage and Use of LPG at Metered Estates" provides further guidance. In this case and where a British Gas mains supply is available, then the Gas Safety (Installation and Use) Regulations 1984 and the Pipe-lines Act 1962 may also be applicable.

Exposed gas bottles or cylinders should not be within the separation boundary of an adjoining unit.

LPG installations should conform to British Standard 5482, "Code of Practice for domestic butane and propane gas burning installations, Part 2: 1977 Installations in Caravans and non-permanent dwellings".

For mains gas supply, the 1984 Regulations will be relevant for the installation downstream of any service pipe(s) supplying any primary meter(s) and such service pipes are subject to the Gas Safety Regulations 1972.

In cases where the site owner supplies gas to caravans on the site, he may need an authorisation to do so from OFGAS under the Gas Act 1986.

Electrical Installations
17. Sites should be provided with an electricity supply sufficient in all respects to meet all reasonable demands of the caravans situated on them.

18. Such electrical installations, other than Electricity Board works and circuits subject to regulations made by the Secretary of State under section 16 of the Energy Act 1983 and section 64 of the Electricity Act 1947, should be installed, tested and maintained in accordance with the provisions of the Institution of Electrical Engineers' (IEE)

Regulations for Electrical Installations for the time being in force, and where appropriate, to the standard which would be acceptable for the purposes of the Electricity (Overhead Lines) Regulations 1988, Statutory Instrument 1988 No. 1057.

19. Work on electrical installations and appliances should be carried out only by competent persons such as the manufacturer's appointed agent, the electricity supplier, a professionally qualified electrical engineer, a member of the Electrical Contractors' Association, a contractor approved by the National Inspection Council for Electrical Installation Contracting, or a qualified person acting on behalf of one of the above. The installations should be inspected periodically: under IEE Wiring Regulations, every year or such longer period (not exceeding 3 years) as is considered appropriate in each case. When an installation is inspected, it should be judged against the current regulations.

The inspector should, within 1 month of such an inspection, issue an inspection certificate in the form prescribed in the IEE Wiring Regulations which should be retained by the site operator and displayed, supplemented or replaced by subsequent certificates, with the site licence. The cost of the inspection and report should be met by the site operator or licence holder.

20. If an inspection reveals that an installation no longer complies with the regulations extant at the time it was first installed, any deficiencies should be rectified. Any major alterations and extensions to an installation and all parts of the existing installation affected by them should comply with the latest version of the IEE Wiring Regulations.

21. If there are overhead electric lines on the site, suitable warning notices should be displayed at the entrance to the site and on supports for the line. Where appropriate, particular attention should be drawn to the danger of masts of yachts or dinghies contacting the line.

Water Supply

22. All sites should be provided with a water supply in accordance with appropriate Water Byelaws and statutory quality standards.

Drainage, Sanitation and Washing Facilities

23. Satisfactory provision should be made for foul drainage, either by connection to a public sewer or sewage treatment works or by discharge to a properly constructed septic tank or cesspool approved by the local authority.

24. Properly designed disposal points for the contents of chemical closets should be provided, with an adequate supply of water for cleaning the containers.

25. For caravans without their own water supply and water closets, communal toilet blocks should be provided, with adequate supplies of water, on at least the following scales:

Men: 1 WC and 1 urinal per 15 caravans.

Women: 2 WCs per 15 caravans.

1 wash basin for each WC or group of WCs.

1 shower or bath (with hot and cold water) for each sex per 20 caravans.

Toilet blocks should be sited conveniently so that all site occupants may have reasonable access to one by means of a road or footpath.

Refuse Disposal

26. Every caravan standing should have an adequate number of suitable non-combustible refuse bins with close-fitting lids or plastic bags. Arrangements should be made for the bins to be emptied regularly. Where communal refuse bins are also provided these should be of similar construction and housed within a properly constructed bin store.

Parking

27. One car only may be parked between adjoining caravans provided that the door to the caravan is not obstructed. Suitably surfaced parking spaces should be provided where necessary to meet the additional requirements of the occupants and their visitors. Plastic or wooden boats should not be parked between units.

Recreation Space

28. Where children stay on the site, space equivalent to about one-tenth of the total area should be allocated for children's games and/or other recreational purposes. This provision will normally be necessary because of the limited space available round the caravans, but may be omitted where there are suitable alternative publicly provided recreational facilities which are readily accessible.

Notices

29. A suitable sign should be prominently displayed at the site entrance indicating the name of the site.

30. A copy of the site licence with its conditions should be displayed prominently on the site.

31. Notices and a plan should be displayed on the site setting out the action to be taken in the event of an emergency. They should show where the police, fire brigade, ambulance, and local doctors can be contacted, and the location of the nearest public telephone. The notices should also give the name and location/telephone number of the site licence holder or his/her accredited representative. At sites subject to flood risk, warning notices should be displayed giving advice about the operation of the flood warning system.

32. All notices should be suitably protected from the weather and displayed where possible out of the direct rays of the sun, preferably in areas lit by artificial lighting.

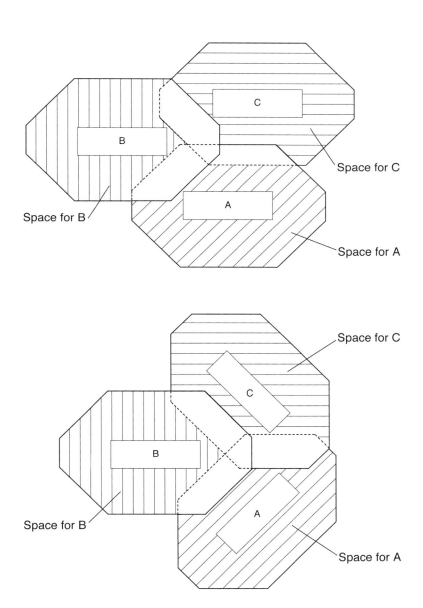

Appendix 1 – Holiday caravan layouts

Appendix C

WRITTEN STATEMENT UNDER THE MOBILE HOMES ACT 1983

as prescribed by the Mobile Homes (Written Statement) Regulations 1983 (S.I. 1983 No. 1749)

IMPORTANT – PLEASE READ THIS STATEMENT CAREFULLY AND KEEP IT IN A SAFE PLACE. IT SETS OUT THE TERMS ON WHICH YOU ARE ENTITLED TO KEEP YOUR MOBILE HOME ON SITE AND TELLS YOU ABOUT THE RIGHTS GIVEN YOU BY LAW. IF THERE IS ANYTHING YOU DO NOT UNDERSTAND YOU SHOULD GET ADVICE (FOR EXAMPLE FROM A SOLICITOR OR A CITIZENS ADVICE BUREAU).

Part I

1. You have an agreement to which the Mobile Homes Act 1983 applies.

2. The parties to the agreement are–

    ....

    ....
    (name and address of mobile home occupier)

    ....

    ....
    (name and address of site owner)

3. The agreement commenced on ....
    (fill in date)

4. The particulars of the land on which you are entitled to station your mobile home are ....

    ....

184

5. The site owner's estate or interest in the land will end on

    .... ; or
    (fill in date)

    The site owner's planning permission for the site will

    end on ....
    (fill in date)

    This means that your right to stay on the site will not continue after that date unless the site owner's interest or planning permission is extended.

Part II
INFORMATION

1. Because you have an agreement with a site owner which entitles you to keep your mobile home on his site and live in it as your home, the Mobile Homes Act 1983 gives you certain rights, affecting in particular your security of tenure and the sale of your mobile home.

2. These rights, which are contained in the implied terms set out in Part III of this statement, apply automatically and cannot be overridden, so long as your agreement continues to be one to which this Act applies.

3. A full explanation of your rights can be found in the booklet "Mobile Homes" produced jointly by the Department for Transport, Local Government and the Regions [now the Office of the Deputy Prime Minister], the Office of the National Assembly for Wales and the Scottish Executive Development Department. The booklet is available free from Council offices and housing aid centres and you are advised to read it.

4. If you are not sure what any of the terms of your agreement mean or how they will work in future, you

should get advice at once from a solicitor or citizens advice bureau.

5. If you are not happy with any of the express terms of your agreement (as set out in Part IV of this statement) you should discuss them with the site owner, who may agree to change them. But if you are still not satisfied you can challenge the agreement in two ways, as explained in paragraphs 6 to 9 below, provided you do so within 6 months of the time you are given this statement.

6. A challenge can be made either in the county court (in Scotland, the sheriff court) or before an arbitrator (in Scotland, an arbiter). You can–

    (a) ask for any of the express terms of the agreement (those set out in Part IV of this statement) to be changed or deleted;

    (b) ask for further terms to be included in the agreement concerning the matters set out in Part II of Schedule 1 to the Act (see paragraph 9 below).

    The site owner can also go to court or to an arbitrator to ask for the agreement to be changed in these two ways.

7. The appointment of an arbitrator may be provided for in one of the express terms of the agreement. If not, you and the site owner can still agree in writing to appoint an arbitrator to settle a dispute between you.

8. The court or the arbitrator must make an order on terms they consider just and equitable in the circumstances. If you wish to challenge your agreement, you should get advice from a solicitor or citizens advice bureau.

9. The matters set out in Part II of Schedule 1 to the Act are as follows–

(a) the right of the occupier to quiet enjoyment, or in Scotland, undisturbed possession of the mobile home;

(b) the sums payable by the occupier in pursuance of the agreement and the times at which they are to be paid;

(c) the review at yearly intervals of the sums so payable;

(d) the provision or improvement of services available on the protected site, and the use by the occupier of such services;

(e) the preservation of the amenity of the protected site;

(f) the maintenance and repair of the protected site by the owner, and the maintenance and repair of the mobile home by the occupier;

(g) access by the owner to the land on which the occupier is entitled to station the mobile home.

10. If no application to court or an arbitrator is made within the six months time limit, both you and the site owner will be bound by the terms of the agreement and will not be able to change them unless both parties agree.

Part III
IMPLIED TERMS
Under the Act, certain terms must be contained in your agreement. This part of the statement sets out those terms.

Duration of agreement
1. Subject to paragraph 2 below, the right to station the mobile home on land forming part of the protected site shall subsist until the agreement is determined under paragraph 3, 4, 5 or 6 below.

2.   (1) If the owner's estate or interest is insufficient to enable him to grant the right for an indefinite period, the period for which the right subsists shall not extend beyond the date when the owner's estate or interest determines.

(2) If planning permission for the use of the protected site as a site for mobile homes has been granted in terms such that it will expire at the end of a specified period, the period for which the right subsists shall not extend beyond the date when the planning permission expires.

(3) If before the end of a period determined by this paragraph there is a change in circumstances which allows a longer period, account shall be taken of that change.

Termination by occupier

3.   The occupier shall be entitled to terminate the agreement by notice in writing given to the owner not less than four weeks before the date on which it is to take effect.

Termination by owner

4.   The owner shall be entitled to terminate the agreement forthwith, if, on the application of the owner, the court–

(a) is satisfied that the occupier has breached a term of the agreement and, after service of a notice to remedy the breach, has not complied with the notice within a reasonable time; and

(b) considers it reasonable for the agreement to be terminated.

5.   The owner shall be entitled to terminate the agreement forthwith if, on the application of the owner, the court is satisfied that the occupier is not occupying the mobile home as his only or main residence.

6.   (1) The owner shall be entitled to terminate the agreement at the end of a relevant period if, on the application of the owner, the court is satisfied that, having regard to its age and condition, the mobile home–

(a) is having a detrimental effect on the amenity of the site; or

(b) is likely to have such an effect before the end of the next relevant period.

(2) In sub-paragraph (1) above, the "relevant period" means the period of five years beginning with the commencement of the agreement and each succeeding period of five years.

Recovery of overpayments by occupier
7.   Where the agreement is terminated as mentioned in paragraph 3, 4, 5 or 6 above, the occupier shall be entitled to recover from the owner so much of any payment made by him in pursuance of the agreement as is attributable to a period beginning after the termination.

Sale of the mobile home
8.   (1) The occupier shall be entitled to sell the mobile home and to assign the agreement to a person approved by the owner, whose approval shall not be unreasonably withheld.

(2) Where the occupier sells the mobile home, and assigns the agreement, as mentioned in sub-paragraph (1) above, the owner shall be entitled to receive a commission on the sale at a rate not exceeding such rate as may be specified by an order made by the Secretary of State.

The maximum rate is presently fixed at 10% by the Mobile Homes (Commissions) Order 1983 (S.I. 1983 No. 748).

Gift of mobile home

9. The occupier shall be entitled to give the mobile home, and to assign the agreement, to a member of his family approved by the owner, whose approval shall not be unreasonably withheld.

Re-siting of mobile home

10. If the owner is entitled to require that the occupier's right to station the mobile home shall be exercisable for any period in relation to other land forming part of the protected site–

    (a) that other land shall be broadly comparable to the land on which the occupier was originally entitled to station the mobile home; and

    (b) all costs and expenses incurred in consequence of the requirement shall be paid by the owner.

Part IV
EXPRESS TERMS OF THE AGREEMENT

This part of the statement sets out the terms of the agreement settled between you and the site owner in addition to the implied terms.

Terms to be filled in by site owner.

INDEX

definitions (cont.)
    statutory nuisances 77
    trailers 151
    widows and widowers 101-02
density and space between caravans 164-65, 174-75
development
    see also planning permission
    certificate of lawful development 66-67
    definition 6, 26
direction indicators 156
disabled, ramps for 164-65, 175
disputes procedures 125, 126-27
    additional terms 125, 126
    arbitration 127-28
    county courts 127-28
    express terms 118-19
    termination by site owner 121-25
    written statements 125
drainage 170-71, 181
drainpipes 164, 174
driving licence requirements 158
dwelling houses
    and capital gains 12
    curtilage use 21, 53
    definitions 132-33

eaves 164, 175
electrical installations
    competent persons 169, 180
    inspection 170, 180
    overhead lines 170, 180
    regulations 169, 179-80
enforcement notices
    discretion 59-60
    persons on whom served 60-61
    powers to serve 59-63
    requirements 62-63
    time limits 61-62
enforcement of planning permission
    see also enforcement notices
    appeals 65-66
    certificate of lawful use or development 66-67
    of conditions 64-65
    injunctions 65
    planning contravention notice 58-59
    stop notices 63-64